There Will Be Cyberwar
How the Move to Network-Centric Warfighting Set
The Stage For Cyberwar

Richard Stiennon

IT-Harvest Press

1221 Bowers, #1274, Birmingham, MI 48009

www.it-harvest.com

ISBN-13: 978-0-9854607-8-5

To the memory of O. Arthur Stiennon
Who taught me perseverance and independence.

THERE WILL BE CYBERWAR

Table of Contents

CHAPTER ONE

Prelude Taiwan Straits......................................1

CHAPTER TWO

Cautionary Tale......................................11

CHAPTER THREE

How We Got Here......................................20

CHAPTER FOUR

Technology Proceeds War......................................41

CHAPTER FIVE

Internet Boom Times......................................50

CHAPTER SIX

First Gulf War......................................53

CHAPTER SEVEN

Cebrowski Force Transformation......................................56

CHAPTER EIGHT

The Rise of CYBERCOM......................................61

CHAPTER NINE

NSA Cyber War Footing......................................67

CHAPTER TEN

Assurance......................................78

CHAPTER ELEVEN

Military Cyber Failures......................................88

CHAPTER TWELVE

Systems Thinking...92

CHAPTER THIRTEEN

Electronic Warfare...94

CHAPTER FOURTEEN

Gathering Cyber Storm....................................98

CHAPTER FIFTEEN

Looking Back, Looking Forward......................102

CHAPTER SIXTEEN

The Dangers of Risk Management.................114

CHAPTER SEVENTEEN

Threat Management.......................................121

CHAPTER EIGHTEEN

Conclusion..135

ACNOWLEGEMENTS

...................................137

NOTES

...................................139

CHAPTER ONE

Prelude Taiwan Straits

REPORT ON SPECIAL INVESTIGATION INTO THE TAIWAN STRAITS CONFLICT OF MARCH 18, 2018
Presented to the Armed Services Sub-Committee May 12, 2018

SUMMARY

This report was commissioned by the Armed Services Committee On The Taiwan Straits Crisis. The bi-cameral Committee, with the support of both the House Permanent Select Committee on Intelligence and the Senate Committee on Armed Services requested an examination of the causes of the first military defeat in battle since Fire Support Base Ripcord in 1970 and the most serious failure since Pearl Harbor. It is not the intent of this investigation to assign blame to individuals as that inquiry is still under way among the service branches. Rather, it is the purpose of this investigation to discover the exact means that an adversary used to surprise the Navy, overwhelm command and control communications channels, negate or redirect missile flights, commandeer the navigation systems of carrier launched fighter jets and supporting tankers, introduce the fog of war, and mislead the Intelligence Services as to intent, to gain overwhelming advantage in battle and ultimately defeat the United States Armed Forces. The shift in regional balance represented by the re-unification of Taiwan with the PRC is one of the consequences of the loss.

This report is preliminary and delivered as-is in light of the serious findings that point to multiple deficiencies in the Department of Defense's ability to field a fighting force against technically advanced adversaries. In addition, recommendations are made for an immediate halt to all weapons systems development until the means are determined to ensure that they can be deployed to full operational ability without experiencing the vulnerabilities that this investigation has discovered. There is also immediate need for a program to remediate already deployed communications systems, target acquisition technology, radar systems, flight hardware and software, and Intelligence, Surveillance, and Reconnaissance (ISR) platforms.

In the lead up to the visit to Washington, DC, by the new President of Taiwan, Chinese officials made it clear that this overture from Taiwan would be viewed as counterproductive to ongoing talks to resolve multiple issues in the region, including the tensions arising with Japan, Viet Nam, and Taiwan over Chinese commencement of extensive oil and gas development in the South China Sea. This development, which includes the first oil rigs delivering crude oil to the refinery built on an artificial island, only added to tensions that had been building since China began harvesting rare earth minerals from the waters West of Hawaii. The bellicose language used by the newly elected President of Taiwan during his campaign, the diplomatic overtures to Japan and the sale of advanced radar systems to Taipei were also contributing factors to the tense situation. Yet US intelligence failed to report on military maneuvers, or any other sign of intent on the part of China to engage militarily with the US. There is strong indication that the NSA and others had been misled over at least 15 years as to the Chinese purpose for its widespread hacking of defense industrial base networks and US military networks. While stealing designs of advanced military systems such as the Joint Strike Fighter and other weapons platforms was evident, it was not clear that the purpose was to discover weaknesses in those systems that the People's Liberation Army could exploit in conflict. While the knowledge that source code and configuration data was stolen was recognized by the NSA and FBI, they never surmised anything beyond industrial espionage.

Since at least 2013, the Chinese PLA had enhanced their use of encryption and embarked on a secret mission to gain advantage over the US fighting forces. It now appears that the entire scenario was planned for years and that, when the time was right, it was executed. It is outside the scope of this report to address the intelligence failure beyond these findings and to recommend a separate investigation into the IC which has focused on data gathering and mining at the expense of long term discovery of adversary intent.

Because of the loud outcry from the Chinese Communist Party and expressions of discomfort from allies in Asia, namely Japan, and Korea, the President asked the Joint Chiefs for guidance. The Joint Chiefs recommended a show of force, which included moving the 7th Fleet into the Taiwan Straits, as well as mobilizing the 4th Fleet from San Diego where it had just returned from the joint US-Korea naval exercises. Diplomatic channels were used to warn China not to move missile barrages into place across the Straits, and apprised Chinese leaders that this was a show of force, not an imminent military incursion. China acknowledged this; however, through channels, added a warning that an incursion into its territorial waters for any reason would be viewed as an act of war.

The investigators who have assembled this report were most

interested in how the 7th Fleet came to encroach on China's territory although the mission plan explicitly called for that boundary to be given a wide berth.

While the inadvertent incursion into Chinese territory is viewed widely as the trigger of the event, this investigation has found that it started days before and that the incursion was manufactured by Chinese action. Every communication channel from the office of POTUS to the Joint Chiefs to Pacific Command was compromised. Not only could the PLA intercept and decrypt those channels, it could also inject misleading information. Work is still under way to determine the implications of the false weather reports that led the commander of the Fleet to understand that weather in the target zone would be clear when in fact it was overcast with limited visibility. Recorded data from most communications during the 72-hour period of the engagement is, of course, missing since it was erased by the infected payloads received.

It now appears that the incident in northern Wisconsin involving what was thought to be a rogue terrorist cell and the death of two DISA officers who were inspecting the ELF array was connected to the events of March. Key management for the US ballistic missile fleet is archaic. While Cold War era means of cycling through encryption keys manually and only periodically sufficed in an earlier period, they evidently should be updated. The attack and loss of the key storage unit that was in the possession of the two officers now appears to have been timed to give the attackers maximum benefit of the encryption keys before they were set to expire. That expiration date, only two days after the engagement, indicates that the PLA had orchestrated the entire set of events, perhaps even inciting the rhetoric around the Taiwan election.

It also now appears that some of the delays experienced by the prime contractor for the GPS III series of satellites was also orchestrated by the PLA. Multiple cyber incursions, which were attributed at the time to DPRK, against subcontractors of critical components set back final delivery by 18 months after two years of delays that can be accounted for by nominal issues with the defense procurement process. In addition the failure of the Delta IV launch vehicle at Vandenberg in January put that launcher on hold pending the accident investigation. In light of the findings in this report it is recommended that the inquiry be expanded to include foul play on the part of foreign agents.

Without the completion of the GPS III constellation the 7th fleet relied on current GPS. The PLA used their own satellites, which had been identified as new weather and earth resource platforms to send signals that were much stronger than the US GPS satellites. These signals are the primary measure the PLA used to set their plan in motion.

As the 7th fleet approached Taiwan it launched four F-35 Lightning fighters. These fighters failed to rendezvous with their tankers. It is evident that their GPS guidance was compromised and they received the wrong coordinates for the rendezvous. At the same time the tankers that had flown from Kunsan Air Base in South Korea were also misguided. The discrepancy between courses is estimated to have been 200 nautical miles. The tankers were able to re-establish correct GPS connections shortly after they left the engagement area. None of their communications reached the 7th Fleet. Low on fuel and headed back to the carrier group the F-35 squadron were intercepted by still unidentified fighter jets. The sole survivor of the trailing F-35 reports that the sophisticated enemy identification systems on board failed to trigger any alerts. Investigations are ongoing but it now appears that the mission data set uploaded to the onboard computers during the flight preparation procedure were corrupted. The entire US Reprogramming Lab at Elgin Air Force Base, Florida, is under investigation as the most likely source of the corrupted data sets.

The loss of communication with the fighters and tankers led the Fleet Commander to believe that he was engaged in an active battle situation and he took steps to arm the Aegis missile systems. Reports from survivors indicate there were no anomalies in the behavior of the Aegis system, all readouts were nominal.

The errant GPS signals were also the cause for the fleet being out of position by 160 nautical miles, putting them well inside the air defense identification zone (ADIZ), China had declared over the East China Sea in November 2013. The overcast skies prevented the normal navigational sightings that may have warned the officers of a problem with the GPS navigation system. Television broadcasts from an island north of Taiwan provided visual confirmation of the fleet being well within China territorial waters. It now appears that the fleet was expected and that the cameras had been positioned specifically to support China's claims of legal authority to strike. Satcoms and imagery did not give warning and may have also been tampered with. The low ceiling and false weather reports contributed to the confusion as Fleet Command tried to regain situational awareness, as they were in a state of disarray trying to ascertain what had happened to the fighter squadron.

When the first Chinese J8 fighters flew a reconnaissance pass it was discovered that the targeting radar systems would not lock on to them. When the torpedo-armed bombers approached, the Commander ordered the launch of Aegis surface-to-air-missiles. These missiles also failed to obtain a lock in-flight and never corrected course. It now appears that the media reports, gathered from the survivors recounting what they had seen, were incorrect. The Chinese aircraft did not have a new stealth technology that made them invisible to radar, but in fact used electronic countermeasures that triggered a previously unknown bug in the radar control systems that caused them to disable the Aegis guidance system.

Coincident with the beginnings of hostilities the USS *Minnesota* (SSN-783) received an unauthorized command via ELF to surface immediately for further instructions. Its mission had been to cover the 7th Fleet and provide support should it be needed. It surfaced well within the radius of effects caused by the upper atmosphere EMP device detonated over the area. Those effects were the first indication that PACCOM had that a major military engagement was under way.

The loss of the USS *Reagan* aircraft carrier and the flanking destroyers was accomplished with Chinese air launched torpedoes. Witnesses from the tenders and other locally-based boats that eventually fled the area report that the carrier and destroyers did not take evasive maneuvers or launch any type of defense. Most of the surface fleet reported loss of radar, ship-to-shore comms, and that onboard systems crashed and were re-booting even as the torpedoes struck. The EMP blast finished what the onboard failures had started, the complete disarming of the 7th Fleet.

There is still no evidence that China launched the nuclear EMP device from the land or sea. It is now apparent that one and possible more of China's satellites were armed with nuclear warheads capable of being launched with precision and guided to an exact upper atmosphere location for detonation. The committee views this capability as destabilizing and counter measures should be developed while ongoing diplomatic pressure brought to bear to stop the militarization of space.

In less than 45 minutes since the fighter squadron launched within China territorial waters, the 7th fleet was disabled, and the USS *Minnesota* was rendered inoperable, which apparently was calculated on the part of China to ensure that no deterrent force was left to interfere with the Chinese ultimate goal: the re-unification of Taiwan. That process was facilitated by the complete power and communication grid failure across Taiwan, leaving them in a state of turmoil as China immediately gained control of the air and sea domain around Taiwan. Once it was evident to Chinese leaders that the 7th Fleet was effectively destroyed the Taiwanese President had no option but to surrender. His fate, upon returning to Taipei, as well as that of his cabinet, are still unknown.

The capitulation of Taiwan and subsequent reunification marks the greatest setback for the United States in the region since the loss of South Viet Nam. The economic impact could be much greater because the future of trade with Taiwan, let alone China, is in doubt. The repercussions throughout the Pacific Rim will be long lasting. The peaceful overtures to China from Japan, Korea, and even Australia's new labor government marks the end of the Obama initiated pivot to Asia.

The committee convened to investigate this military defeat can point to several underlying causes.

1. The most important factor was the misreading of China's intentions. The West in general and the US in particular had moved ahead with economic development and normalization with the Communist-led state based on incorrect assumptions about the inevitability of advanced nations moving towards liberal democracy. Despite many researchers and China experts' warnings about China's long-term, even 100 year goals, warnings

were dismissed. From the perspective of a liberal democracy where long-term planning rarely surpasses the next election cycle, execution of a strategy over more than 20 years is hard to comprehend. Yet, that strategy was well documented in Chinese academic and military writings, especially the use of cyber attack to gain asymmetric advantage in battle.

2. The DoD, while investing heavily in network defenses and its own cyber attack capabilities, led by the 2010 formation of US Cyber Command, completely overlooked the vulnerability of its own platforms for communication, precision targeting, guidance and navigation, and ISR.

3. The NSA had used network intrusions against the Defense Industrial Base to further its own buildup of cyber capacity but never reported all of its findings to Congress. In particular, the concerted effort of PLA cyber teams to find and exfiltrate the source code and technical configurations of radar, sensing platforms, targeting platforms, and encryption key distribution methods was omitted from reports. This targeting, if properly reported, would have been the first indicator of China's intentions for future war fighting.

4. The billions of dollars invested in cyber defense since 2008 were primarily applied to operational networking and email systems. No thought was given to hardening weapons platforms against cyber attacks.

The investigation committee recommends:

1. All weapons development programs be halted immediately and a software and vulnerability review be instituted across all logistics, re-supply, aircraft, ships, and combat gear that has the ability to network or receive instructions via any electromagnetic

means.

2. A supply chain review should be made of all components. A process should be implemented to detect tampering and installation of back doors, particularly those manufactured in China. Logistics controls should be developed and applied to protect any critical gear from interdiction.

2. Every device and piece of communications gear that encrypts data should be re-keyed immediately.

3. A key distribution and management system that is not highly centralized must be developed and deployed as soon as possible.

4. Strong means of authenticating GPS signals must be developed and deployed as soon as possible.

5. The placement of nuclear devices in orbit by China is being taken to the UN Security Council. In the meantime effective means of anti-satellite defenses must be developed to prevent a future occurrence of space delivered nuclear weapons with guided, hypersonic re-entry vehicles.

6. The DoD should undergo a top down review of its command structure, procurement processes, and ability to project force in the face of a new reality.

CHAPTER TWO

Cautionary Tale

The foregoing fictional scenario is meant purely as an exercise in predicting the worst case outcome of a situation that has evolved over the past two decades. The US military, and indeed most advanced military organizations, have moved to a network-centric war fighting stance with little or no thought, until very recently,[1] to the incumbent vulnerabilities that entails.

In 2011 Leon Panetta, then US Secretary of Defense, joined the chorus of those newly awakened to the reality of the threat of cyber attack against critical infrastructure when he warned of an impending "cyber Pearl Harbor." But Panetta got his metaphor wrong. An attack against critical infrastructure of the type he and many Cassandras rail on about, one that shuts down the power and communication grids, would be more akin to a terrorist attack than a military surprise attack. The metaphor Panetta should have used was a "cyber 9/11." A "cyber Pearl Harbor," if the metaphor were to be correctly applied, would entail a military defeat via cyber means, which the previous chapter attempted to dramatize. In other words, an adversary's use of computer network attack (CNA) and exploitation (CNE) to gain a tactical advantage that leads to a lost battle, a change in military standing, or even a shift in the geopolitical balance, would be most comparable to the destruction of the Pacific Fleet at Pearl Harbor, on December 7, 1941.

This book takes us on a journey from the development of the

Internet, to the exciting days of the new information age, and then to the discovery of the power of networking by the US military. The history of the development of attacks against vulnerabilities in the commercial world has a parallel in the domain of governments, militaries, and war fighting; a parallel that allows us to project into the future. That future vision includes a humiliating military defeat at the hands of a more capable digital adversary. One such scenario, played out in the introduction, was chosen for a particular reason.

The 1995-96 Taiwan Straits Crisis

The history of China and Taiwan is short and consistent. When Mao Zedong finally won the Communist revolution against the Chinese Nationalists in 1949, Chiang Kai-Shek fled with his forces to the adjacent island of Formosa and established a new country, Taiwan. Since then China's stated goal has been to reunify the two countries. Whether it will be a peaceful reunification (like that of Hong Kong in 1999) or a violent reunification, contributes to the long lasting tension between the two countries. During the Korean War there were multiple armed invasions of Taiwan from China.

In 1991 Taiwanese President Lee Teng-hui angered China with his statements about reunification, leaning away from the One China rhetoric that both countries generally stuck to. Then in 1994 Lee was traveling from South America when his flight was diverted to Honolulu to refuel. The Clinton Administration, cognizant of the delicate situation, bowed to Chinese pressure and refused to grant Lee a visa, forcing him to stay overnight in the plane. Tensions began to rise in 1995 when Lee was invited to speak at his Alma Mater, Cornell University. Congress passed a resolution requiring the State Department to grant him a visa. This was during the lead up to the first fully democratic presidential elections in Taiwan and China took a dim view of the situation. Lee spoke at Cornell in June 1995.

China announced missile tests in a region near Taiwan and began maneuvers on the mainland across the Straits from Taiwan in Fujian Provence. They carried out a series of missile launches into the sea to the North of Taiwan in July. The Clinton Administration took steps to demonstrate that the United States was willing to intercede if China threatened an invasion. In March of 1996 two aircraft carrier battle groups were deployed to the vicinity.

This is where Admiral Archie Clemins comes into the story. Clemins was the Vice Admiral of the US Navy's 7th Fleet. Only two years before, upon achieving flag rank, he had been assigned to the training division of the US Pacific Fleet under Admiral Frank Kelso. He was also dual-hatted as head of N6, the information technology arm of the Pacific Fleet.

As an "IT guy," Clemins began to carry a laptop with him, an unusual sight in the 1993 Navy. It was an Apple PowerBook, probably a 160 with 4 MB of memory and a 40 MB hard drive. It was one of the earliest flip top portable computers and had a grayscale LCD screen. It weighed 6.8 pounds.

His Powerbook was his constant companion, even on trips to the Pentagon. He found that people, specifically Admiral Robert J. Kelly, Commander of the Pacific Fleet based in Hawaii, were asking him for copies of the notes he took on his portable. He was living the Information Revolution of the time. "That started the use of computers, we, at Training Group Pacific, led everybody, with desktop computers."[2]

Shortly after taking on the Pacific Fleet role based in San Diego, Admiral Clemins got a call from the Navy's Assignment

Officer who asked how he liked the weather in San Diego and if he would like to transfer to the Pentagon? The previous week Admiral Keslo, head of Naval Operations, had announced a major reorganization of the Navy and Clemins had been chosen to lead the effort.

As Clemins pulled together a small team within the Pentagon he made sure that they used technology to its best advantage. Clemins credits this use of computers for the success his team had in accomplishing the Navy reorganization in 12 months instead of the 18 months originally slated for it.

Clemins was then appointed Deputy Commander of the Atlantic Fleet at Norfolk to accomplish the same reorganization. "The more I did this the more I came to believe this [computer technology] was the way we were going."

From Norfolk, Clemins was promoted to commander of the 7th Fleet where he had served as chief of staff years before. He was determined to bring the fleet into the Information Age: "You have to remember the ships of the time, '93-94 are still moving information at teletype speed." That meant at most 80 messages a day of 40 lines each. All messages would go directly to the Commanding Officer (CO) who would route them to the appropriate department or personnel.

Clemins' first task was to assemble a team. He drew from surface, air, and submarine commanders. This was 1995, the year Windows 95 came out, the first commercial operating system with embedded TCP/IP networking capability. Mark Lenci, the submarine captain that Clemins tasked with retrofitting the 7th Fleet, had little experience with networking. His only qualification: he had an AOL account. But no one in the command ranks was an expert and Clemins chose a team that could learn quickly and get things done. When Lanci reported to duty aboard Clemin's command ship, the USS *Blue Ridge*, he recalls Clemins saying "let's go take a walk." On the flight deck he explained his vision of NCW. "I don't know what a WAN (wide area network) is but I know we need one. Get the smart guys together here in the Pacific. We are going to do it." And they were going to do it with commercial off the shelf products (COTS). [3]

The Blue Ridge, the command ship of the 7th Fleet, was the first to be outfitted. Lenci relates how welders were sent on board to cut out bulkheads and toss them into the South China Sea as the Blue Ridge was steaming to port. Ships of the day had stove piped IT infrastructure. Every agency or group that needed computing power deployed their own complete stack of equipment and satellite communication gear. None of the 48 systems, all running different flavors of Unix, could interoperate and none of his team knew how to run them. The satellite antenna system looked "like a pop can with a bundle of straws strapped to it" Lenci recalls.[3]

Lenci was deployed to Washington to scrounge funds from "end of the year" money available from budgets that had not been fully spent. He returned to Japan with $4 million available for the retrofit. He and his team began to outfit both the Blue Ridge and the aircraft carrier USS *Independence* with a network of Windows 95 machines. Finding bandwidth on satellite comm links proved to be difficult. Most links were controlled by the intelligence agencies and they did not want to cooperate.

So Lenci, who had spent some time at SPAWAR (Space and Naval Warfare Systems Command) called a friend in Cheyenne Mountain. He asked him for a list of all satellite transponders on geo-synchronous orbits over the Pacific theater. Of the list compiled there were seven Inmarsat satellites that were being decommissioned but still had onboard fuel so they could be repositioned. He commandeered these satellites, which to this day are still employed by the US Navy.

In very short order the beginnings of a networked fleet were accomplished. All seven shore bases (including HK, Singapore, Honolulu, and Guam) could communicate via email. The technical barrier to communications had been broken down. But, as usual with change within military structures, the biggest hurdles were getting people to change. The COs could not get comfortable with everyone in their command being able to communicate with anyone on shore or another ship. They insisted that all emails be sent to them, printed out, and distributed in the old way.

To counter this, Admiral Clemins had an "Eyes Only" email sent to each of his seven one-star admirals. The email requested their presence for an important strategy meeting in Japan. It was a test to see who actually read their email. Only four of the admirals came to the meeting. After that, the COs began to read their emails assiduously.

When China began to bluster over Taiwan, Admiral Clemins's newly deployed systems were put to the test. The planning process for any Navy operation is cumbersome and time consuming. Multiple scenarios are proposed, researched and analyzed. The process can take days and is hampered by the communication at "teletype speeds." When President Clinton ordered the 7th Fleet to send two carrier battle groups to the region, Clemins went into action. The Independence, shore bases, and the command ship were engaged in live communications with the Pentagon. Many options were discussed, even the possible need to enter a harbor in Taiwan. To support the deliberations a young seaman was able to pull up a live feed from a webcam focused on the harbor in question. It is telling of the interagency friction and embedded processes that the intel community objected to using such open-source data. It had not gone through the intelligence cycle–

tasking, collection, analysis and reporting—after all.

At one point, and perhaps for the first time in history, Clemins used a Microsoft PowerPoint presentation, broadcast directly to the Pentagon, to help communicate the tactical situation in the region. He was interrupted by the Chairman of the Joint Chiefs who asked that a copy of the slides be expedited to the Pentagon (meaning put on a plane) Clemins instead asked the Chairman's aide for his email address. Onscreen he pulled down the share menu and sent the PowerPoint to the General. Within minutes an aide had retrieved a hard copy and placed it in front of the General. The Chairman of the Joint Chiefs turned to the other guys, "I want this on every joint command. Now." This was the moment when the military changed forever. Network-Centric war fighting was born.[4]

The USS *Independence* was deployed to within 600 miles of Taiwan while China launched ballistic missiles into target grounds just north and south of the island nation. When the presence of the Independence did not induce the Chinese to communicate, the USS *Nimitz* was ordered to steam from the Gulf towards Taiwan. All of the planning and decision process took hours instead of what would formerly have taken days.

Data of the Chinese missile flights were recorded by the deployed ships. They identified the flight path and type of missile. That data was scheduled to be put on a floppy disk flown via F-14 to shore and from there by air transport back to Washington for analysis. In a brash moment Clemins had Lenci email the file via his AOL account—unencrypted— over Inmarsat and the Internet.

The successful mission deployment during the Taiwan Straits had repercussions geopolitically and for the future of the US and other military organizations.

Geopolitically, the Taiwanese were reassured that the US would stand by them.

And on China's side: Taiwanese researcher Arthur Ding wrote: "After the crisis, China learned one lesson: the US would definitely get involved in a future Taiwan Strait conflict in one way or another, and Beijing had to be prepared as early as possible for different contingencies associated with such a scenario." [5]

The Navy program set in motion by Clemins, called Collaboration At Sea, is still being used. The USS *Blue Ridge* is still there. IT21, the Navy's future plan for NCW was born in the Taiwan Straits Crisis. The Navy Marine Corps Internet was born. Admiral Arthur Cebrowski was bought in to articulate NCW. Admiral Bill Owens, whose son served under Lenci and eventually went on to command his own submarine, became the lead proponent of NCW and the author of *Eliminating the Fog of War* a seminal book on NCW.

Even though the Straits Crises was the most tense use of a show of force between the US and China since the Korean War, the US kept communication channels open with China's leadership throughout. The political spin of the time led even the press to believe that two aircraft carriers had actually been deployed to steam through the Straits. In reality the aircraft carriers, while mobilized, did not intrude on China's territorial waters and stayed well clear of the missile ranges. Similar to a chess game where two rooks are moved to dominate strategic ranks and files, the fleet movements demonstrated capability more than an actual threat.

Using the Taiwan Straits crisis as a foil for presenting a future re-enactment induced by China is not the main point of this book. The point is the impact on military thinking–on all sides–from the introduction of networking to military operations.

It is not the destruction of the power grid, or the loss of

communications from attacks against the Internet and telecom infrastructure, or even the collapse of the stock market that deserves Panetta's dire warning. Only a crippling military defeat thanks to overwhelming control of the cyber domain deserves to be labeled a Cyber Pearl Harbor. As we will see, the rapid move towards network-nentric warfighting, spawned by Admiral Clemins' entrepreneurial leadership, has mirrored the move to a network-centric economy. Business learned quickly to deploy computers, email, and web browsers to take advantage of the Internet for commerce, communication, even control of critical infrastructure. Just as the business world has had to counter viruses, worms, and targeted attacks, so too has the military had its share of trouble with a networked fighting force.

As the world braces for the fallout of what is being called the Internet of Things (IoT) or as Cisco is branding it, the Internet of Everything (IoE), the military has to prepare for attacks against its "things": Airplanes, ships, tanks, missiles, precision guided munitions, communications, satellites, and drones.

CHAPTER THREE

How We Got Here

It is nearly impossible for humans to forego immediate gratification in the face of imagined future downsides. If this is true on the individual level it is a tendency multiplied by a large factor for organizations like banks, oil and gas refiners, and manufacturers. The largest organizations that are proof of this contention are governments. For them, even certainties like the dire condition of the US Social Security system, or the poor conditions of freeways, bridges, and damns, are continuously pushed into the future. The populace, and their elected representatives, rarely pay attention to future eventualities in the face of present crises.

Before beginning we must take on a few semantic challenges, particularly that of the use of the word *cyber*. It is unfortunate that the government, especially the military, took on a word that meets with so much derision within the technical circles made up of the very people with the skills and knowledge needed to design, build and protect information technology infrastructure.

While the word *cyber* had its genesis in science fiction, its use in military jargon quickly came to mean, in it its broadest sense, computers and the networks that bind them together. As the concept evolved it came to take on those aspects of computing that touched on IT security. The earlier parlance within the military included terms such as Computer Network Attack (CNA) and Computer Network Exploitation (CNE); the latter usually being associated with espionage, but as we will see has become an important aspect of reconnaissance prior to an attack. All of these terms were subsumed both semantically and organizationally into *cyber* and US Cyber Command.

Another problematic word is cyberwar, which has been abused in many ways, just as the terms *trade war, currency war, drug war*, and even *war of words*, have been frequently used to imply a confrontation and escalation of the use of trade sanctions, currency devaluations, countering the drug trade, and heated debate.

In the recently published collection, *Cyber Warfare: A Multidisciplinary Analysis*, the editors adopted the following definition of cyber warfare:

> Cyber warfare is an extension of policy by actions taken in cyberspace by state actors (or by non-state actors with significant state direction or support) that constitute a serious threat to another state's security, or an action of the same nature taken in response to a serious threat to a state's security (actual or perceived).[1]

The The NATO Cooperative Cyber Defense Centre of Excellence (CCDCE) in Tallinn has adopted a definition from the Austrian Cyber Security Strategy document: [2]

> Cyber war refers to acts of war in and around virtual space with means which are predominantly associated with information technology. In a broader sense, this implies the support of military campaigns in traditional operational spaces – i.e. ground, sea, air and outer space – through measures taken in the virtual space. In general, the term also refers to high-tech warfare in the information age based on the extensive computerisation, electronisation and networking of almost all military sectors and issues.[3]

Our task, in describing a future cyberwar, is made much easier if we accept a well constrained definition of cyberwar (and avoid having to define cyberspace or virtual space!):

Cyberwar is the use of computer and network attacks to further the goals of a war-fighting apparatus.

This definition constrains cyberwar to the military use of computer and network attacks (cyber attacks) while leaving open the possibility of non-state actors such as terrorists and violent activists using similar methods to extend their cause. Just as guns, bombs, and missiles can be used in non-warfare violence by criminals, mad men, and terrorists, cyber attacks are used by criminals, hackers, and activists. These threat actors, while extremely important to the development of cyber attack methods and the defenses that have been built to counter them, do not engage in cyberwar. But insurgencies, and transnational terrorist organizations can engage in cyberwar, although they usually do not have the same reliance on technical infrastructure as the states they are fighting against.

Shane Harris, journalist and author of @*War*, argues effectively that the surge and eventual success of the US in the war in Iraq was actually due to cyber war-fighting, going so far as to call it the "first cyberwar." [4] He bases his thesis on the surveillance net that was dropped over all communications in and out of Iraq as well as internal cell phone calls. This capability arose from the post-9/11 surveillance infrastructure built by the NSA. It was re-purposed to build link maps of insurgent cells. Locations of insurgents were betrayed by their use of cell phones, and led to precision targeting of meeting points. Harris claims that false messages were injected into their communications to induce them to walk into traps. He goes on to credit the eventual success of the surge on these cyber means. While this represents an amazing advance in the use of intelligence to wage war it only marginally fits the definition above. Insurgents in Iraq leveraged modern communications (provided by their adversaries) to organize, leaving them open to spying and sabotage. But they also used improvised munitions and relatively non-technical weaponry that were not susceptible to cyber attack. They had no drones, radar, planes, tanks, precision targeting, or satellite reconnaissance. Future cyberwar will involve all of these elements.

Before the term cyberwar was coined the phrase most commonly used was *information warfare.* Now that we have a definition of cyberwar we can allow information warfare to take on the connotation of psychological warfare and disinformation campaigns, such as those so expertly carried out by modern day Russia in concealing its intentions for Ukraine. The use of "armies" of social media commenters has become a weapon of information war fielded by many countries; Russia and China are the most notable examples but even the UK and the US apparently engage in this activity according to Snowden documents. The Kremlin reportedly operates its "troll farm" from 55 Savushkina Street in St. Petersburg according to one confessional.[5] China's effort to sway public perception through social media is termed the "50 Cent Party" in reference to the fee the trolls earn for each post.[6] In February 2015 it was reported that the UK MoD is standing up the 77th battalion which will contain 1,500 "units" responsible for Tweets and Facebook posts to influence outcomes. These "Facebook Warriors" will "wage complex and covert information and subversion campaigns."[7]

Cyber espionage is another term that bears refining. In its broadest sense it means cyber attacks, carried out ultimately by state actors, or at least sponsored by state actors, the purpose of which is to steal information. There can be many motivations for stealing information. Commercial espionage is the most evident with many cases of confidential information being stolen that could help the attacker become more competitive. Stealing designs, processes, and data from a competitor can help a nation's own industry to become more efficient or gain an edge in negotiations over contracts. On the diplomatic and military front there is certainly a free-for-all in espionage as many states engage in cyber spying.

There is one aspect of cyber espionage that will require our attention: espionage carried out to discover the network, computers, and applications within an adversary's infrastructure for the purposes of engaging in targeted attacks. Just as warfare has always involved reconnaissance to discover an enemy's position, forces, and intent, cyber espionage is a necessary component of planning and executing a successful cyber attack. This could be termed *cyber reconnaissance*, or perhaps *cyber recon*.

Now that we are clear on terminology, let us go back to tracing the evolution of cyber attacks, and more importantly, why defenders are always in reaction mode, and very rarely, if ever, invest in defenses *before* an attack. This is an important consideration because we are going to demonstrate that military organizations, particularly the US Department of Defense, are also guilty of this cyber myopia.

The commercial world is arguably as much as a decade ahead of the military when it comes to its experience with hackers, spammers, cyber criminals, and DDoS attacks. Financial institutions, retail, e-commerce, and technology firms have been investing in stronger IT security measures. While generally reactive at least they are keeping up.

The history of IT security failures is replete with examples of myopia when it comes to even the most obvious security controls. Who in IT security has not heard the refrain "but who would attack us, we have nothing worth stealing?" It is only a lack of imagination, perhaps excusable, that supports the conviction that an organization will not be targeted.

Retail

Retailers have suffered many attacks against their Point of Sale (PoS) systems by cyber criminals, even as they took advantage of new technologies like WiFi and the Internet to report store sales to headquarters. Attacks have escalated from physically replacing the card readers with devices that had hardware back doors[8] to infiltrating store locations over open WiFi access points (Lowe's[9], TJX[10]), to the recent massive breach of Target stores where a Heating, Ventilation, and Air Conditioning (HVAC) contractor's credentials were used to gain access and spread malware that captured data from the POS system memory.[11]

The use of credit cards for conducting transactions came with what now appears to be a glaring systemic vulnerability. All a criminal needs to make fraudulent transactions is the credit card number, a 3-4 digit Card Verification Value (cvv) and perhaps the owner's name and address. Before e-commerce a criminal would have to either steal the physical credit card or engage in mail theft to get that information from the customer billing statement, or someone who handled credit cards at a retailer would make copies of the information, or sometimes make multiple charges against the credit card presented. By far the most damaging abuse of credit cards was fraudulent charge backs. Customers would make purchases they could not afford and then deny that they had done so. Merchants did not have the resources to counter all the charge backs and would be left eating the costs while the card holders got to keep their purchases and receive a credit.

As e-commerce and online banking grew, this vulnerability became more and more dangerous, primarily to retail merchants. Their early reactions to cyber crime were slow and nearsighted.

One of the first attacks against a major retailer was that of the Lowe's hack. It is noteworthy in that it highlights the willingness of IT departments to deploy technology for its advantages without any thought for the vulnerabilities it introduces. The technology in question was WiFi. In the early 2000s large retailers took advantage of WiFi in their stores to save on the costs of network cabling and gain advantage from roaming scanners for inventory management. Eventually even Point of Sale terminals (PoS) were connected to the network via WiFi. A young hacker in Michigan took advantage of vulnerabilities in default configurations for these WiFi access points. He and an accomplice sat outside the Lowe's Home Improvement store in Southfield, Michigan with their laptops and a foil covered Pringles can to extend the range of their WiFi antenna. Their goal: steal credit card data from the store network and sell it to Russian organized crime who ran an extensive card fraud network (called "carding" in the criminal world.)

But the FBI had been alerted that Lowe's was experiencing some sort of attack. They had deployed a large team who staked out the physical network drops in the store, not realizing that the attackers were using WiFi. Luckily, an agent deployed to the roof noticed the suspicious car in the parking lot. A Pringles can wrapped in aluminum foil *is* rather conspicuous. The FBI arrested and prosecuted the hackers to great acclaim and positive press. That was 2003.

Four years later TJX Corporation, another large retailer that operated, among others, the Tj Maxx clothing stores, succumbed to the exact same method of attack. A hacker squatting in a parking lot outside the Minneapolis store broke in over insecure WiFi to steal 45.6 million credit cards, the record for the time. TJX did not even know of the successful attack until they were notified by the credit card associations that they were the source of millions of pilfered accounts. Apparently TJX did not recognize the attack against Lowe's as an early warning. Either its executives were oblivious or perhaps thought that, not being a home building supply retailer, the Lowe's attack was not relevant.

Fast forward past the hundreds of ensuing breaches of retailers, payment processors, and banks, to the holiday shopping season in 2013. After ten years retailers were fully aware that protecting customer credit cards was an important responsibility. Perhaps Target Corporation, one of the largest retailers in the world, thought that their investments in security were adequate, although their lack of appreciation of the threat may be evident in the absence of a top security executive. Target had no Chief Information Security Officer (CISO), a title and role that had become near pervasive in financial services since the appointment of the first CISO, Steve Katz in 1995, by CitiGroup.

Only months before Target was targeted, new versions of a type of malware that infected PoS terminals had shown up on the radar of security researchers. Their reports of BlackPoS were widely published. The malware resided in memory on the WindowsXP based cash registers and copied credit and debit card information as the cards were swiped. The malware would then transmit the stolen data to the cyber criminal who had distributed it. In the case of Target the malware was installed via a network connection that belonged to a HVAC contractor, a now classic third party attack vector. Leading up to the busy holiday shopping season that begins the day after Thanksgiving, Target should, in hindsight, have been on high alert. Given the existence of a new attack methodology "in the wild" PoS terminals should have been hardened. Network monitoring for attack and exfiltration should have been deployed. In one of the largest breaches up to that point, 40 million credit cards were stolen. Target has revealed that the cost of cleanup and updating the PoS terminals will exceed $100 million and consented to a $10 million settlement in a class action lawsuit. The CIO and CEO lost their jobs. The new CEO appointed Target's first CISO.

Target was not alone in succumbing to these new attacks, Michaels craft stores suffered a similar breach at the same time and Home Depot (direct competitor of Lowe's) suffered an even greater loss of credit cards in 2014.

The Gemalto findings from the 2014 Data Breach Level Index found:

> There were 176 data breaches among retailers, accounting for 11% of the total, which was up slightly from 8% in 2013. These attacks resulted in more than half a billion (567,316,824) data records being exposed. That amounted to 55% of all the records involved in data breaches during the year, compared with 29% in 2013.[12]

Sadly, investing in security to prevent the increasingly sophisticated attacks against retail operations is always after the fact.

Media

Retailers have been shown over and again to 1) have valuable assets in the form of credit cards, and 2) be unwilling to invest before the threat materializes in the form of a successful breach. Media companies, although thoroughly reporting the rise of cybercrime and nation-state cyber attacks have also been remarkably blind to the threat against their own organizations.

The New York Times has had its share of learning experience when it comes to cybersecurity. In September 1998 its web page was defaced by a hacking group calling itself "Hacking For Girlies." And in 2002 Adrian Lamo, a young hacker who was to become notorious for his part in turning in Bradley (now Chelsea) Manning for leaking State Department cables to Wikileaks in 2010, broke in to *The New York Times* through several proxy servers that had very weak passwords.

These and myriad other attacks against news media should have been a red flag and forewarning of future attacks of a more serious nature: attacks to discover sources, the most closely guarded secrets of a news organization.

The Washington Post discovered a persistent attack that they attributed to China in 2011. *The Post* revealed the attack when *The New York Times* and *Wall Street Journal* reported similar attacks against their systems in February 2013.

Yet, in the wake of reporting on massive corruption within the Chinese Communist Party, *The New York Times* experienced an attack that stole all of its employees' passwords and targeted the journalists responsible for researching and reporting on wealth accumulated by a Chinese official and his family.

"Based on a forensic analysis going back months, it appears

the hackers broke into *The Times's* computers on Sept. 13 [2012], when the reporting for the Wen articles was nearing completion. They set up at least three back doors into users' machines that they used as a digital base camp. From there they snooped around *The Times's* systems for at least two weeks before they identified the domain controller that contains user names and hashed, or scrambled, passwords for every Times employee."[13]

Even after bringing in breach response company Mandiant to help them clean up in 2012, *The New York Times* continues to experience breaches such as those reported in 2013.

Critical Infrastructure

Perhaps the most egregious lack of vision, when it comes to security, is exhibited by operators of power generation and transmission facilities. Loss of their systems would cause cascading financial loss and possibly deaths.

The worst blackout in recent North American history occurred August 14 2003, the same year that saw the spread of multiple worms based on vulnerabilities in Windows products. Code Red, Nimda, MSBlaster, and SQL Slammer were rampant and the operators of the North American grid were not impervious. Of course Windows was used widely at the generation and transmission facilities. And of course those systems were not patched adequately and were eventually shown to have been infected. The final report of the investigation of the incident[14] ran to 238 pages. While the primary cause was identified as a tree branch that had fallen on a power line, the real lesson learned was that the power grid was fragile. This fragility could easily be taken advantage of by attackers, so the need to beef up IT security was strongly identified in 2003.

Yet operators have consistently resisted implementing defenses. When FERC, the Federal Energy Regulatory Commission, asked the operators to identify their critical assets they provided an astounding response: zero. They had zero critical systems. No assets, if disabled by cyber attack, would pose a threat to the power grid. Ten years later, in 2014, the operators had come around to the point where they admitted to 260 critical transformers and power transmission stations. Less than 3% of all facilities.

The writing is on the wall. The power grid will experience a failure due to targeted cyber attack. It may be a mischievous hacker poking around inside an exposed control system and clicking on the wrong button. But it is likely to be an attacker with much more malicious intent.

Here are the elements that serve as forewarning:

1. In 2014 two families of malware were discovered by security researchers that target control systems. Haylox is already widely distributed in North America. It has been shown to be a derivative of SandWorm, a cyber espionage tool that was found throughout European and NATO offices and attributed to Russian sources. The ICS-ISAC, the public/private partnership for sharing and analyzing cyber threats against Industrial Control Systems, issued a warning in the summer of 2014 that a new family of malware, dubbed BlackEnergy, was targeting vulnerabilities in three of the most widely deployed software packages used to manage control systems. Siemens, GE, and Advantech.

Vulnerable systems that are exposed to the Internet are mapped by Shodan.[15]

Initially unreported, but thanks to a German government

report, we now know of the first attack against an industrial control system that caused damage. A German steel plant was attacked and a blast furnace was destroyed.[16]

Widespread vulnerabilities, systems connected to the Internet, exploits in the wild, infected systems identified, and a first use example. Nothing more is needed to predict impeding disaster for the power grid and other critical infrastructure.

Of course there are other operators of critical infrastructure. Oil and gas refining and transport, communications, traffic, train, and air traffic control, hospitals, manufacturers, and prisons, all operate control systems that are poorly air-gapped and even more poorly defended. It is inevitable that attacks against all of these systems will become common. But fair warning has been given.

Function before security

To build the case that rapid adoption of networking capabilities is almost always accompanied by a lack of adequate security, it is valuable to consider the rise of the Internet and its growth in many spaces: consumers, new e-commerce businesses, traditional business such as retail, financial services, law firms, and regrettably, critical infrastructure providers such as electricity, oil and gas, and transportation. In every case the benefits from reaching a global market, fast and simple communications, and inventing new ways to interact with customers has taken precedence over the risk from increased exposure to attacks on those newly extended capabilities.

In practically every case, new capabilities enabled by the Internet are deployed before adequate protections are added. At launch, new services such as Facebook, Twitter, and Gmail do not have value to attackers. But as they grow and become ubiquitous they become very valuable. The lack of adversaries willing to take advantage of insecure systems allows these new capabilities to grow until they become essential to operations, profits, and market success. Only after they become targets are the requisite security measures added.

Today the battle against new vulnerabilities, and malware that exploits them, is not over but it is under control with the emergence of an IT security industry with over $62 billion in annual spending. [17]

As the email systems that provided so much inspiration to Cebrowski in the Taiwan Straits incident became the predominant means of communications around the world, it came with its own scourges: spam, phishing, and the evolution of Advanced Persistent Threats (APT) such as those attributed to Iran in attacks against the Navy Marine Corps Internet (NMCI).[18] That incident involved a malware payload attached to emails that were delivered to individuals within the network. Once installed the malware spread throughout the NMCI and caused a total shutdown for two days.

Banks have also suffered through their own learning curve as they adapted to the information age. Cyber criminals targeted the early users of online banking with phishing emails, which led the unwary to counterfeit sites that would induce them to enter their usernames and passwords. The initial response of US banks was to assure their customers that they would be reimbursed for any losses from cyber theft; a perfect example of treating the symptom instead of the cause. Banks are complicit in the rise of cybercrime. Rather than deploy technologies such as two-factor authentication to increase the costs for the attackers, they did nothing but reduce the risk for their customers. In other words, they felt the costs of deploying security technology, and the danger of turning off customers, was less than the cost of reimbursements for cyber theft. The unintended consequence was that cyber criminals reaped profits from their attacks and continued to develop more and more sophisticated and lucrative attacks against banks.

In the cat-and-mouse game of attackers versus defenders the problem grew to the point where stronger means of authentication were deployed, as cyber criminals escalated their capabilities to include hijacking a session and stealing funds while the user was logged in. They also developed sophisticated malware that acts as a man-in-the-middle to an authenticated session, even inducing the bank customer to download malware to their smart phones so that out-of-band authorization for money transfers was intercepted.[19]

Participants in the US Defense Industrial Base (DIB), like all enterprises, were quick to get online and network their engineering and design offices with the rest of the business organization. On top of that, the entire supply chain was networked leading to more exposure. It was not until the discovery of Titan Rain in 2004 that they began to understand the windfall to industrial-military espionage that the information age represented. The exfiltration of terabytes of data on the F-35 Joint Strike Fighter (JSF) was widely cited when it occurred in 2008 as the greatest loss of military technical information reported up to that time. According to *The Wall Street Journal* "The intruders appear to have been interested in data about the design of the plane, its performance statistics and its electronic systems, former officials said."[20] More attacks on the DIB were reported by the Defense Science Board in 2013. Design data was stolen for a long list of weapons platforms including: Patriot missile PAC-3 system, the Terminal High Altitude Area Defense (THAAD), the Aegis ballistic-missile defense system, F/A-18 fighter jet, the V-22 Osprey, the Black Hawk helicopter and the Navy's new Littoral Combat Ship.[21]

The Pentagon too, in its rush to form a NCW capability has demonstrated that they did not deploy adequate defenses. The reported incidents of successful attacks against military networks raises the concern that the vaunted capabilities of NCW were deployed without the appropriate concern for protecting the inherent vulnerabilities in those systems.

History of cyber incursions

To build on the thesis that the military rushed to network its systems without concern for cyber vulnerability it is only necessary to review the recent history of successful incursions into the operational side of DoD. From reviewing military documents and noting their lack of requirements for end-to-end security, it is possible to make the assumption that weapons systems, battle management systems, command and control networks, and ISR communications also lack in basic security precautions against determined attackers.

Of those that have been publicized, the attacks that became known under the code name Titan Rain demonstrate that China was engaging in cyber espionage to gain access to military research institutes and labs as early as 2004. Sandia Labs, Redstone Arsenal, NASA and the World Bank were just some of sites that had experienced exfiltration of documents as discovered by Shawn Carpenter, an intrusion detection analyst at Sandia Labs, a division of defense contractor Lockheed Martin.[22]

In 2007 the Pentagon revealed that its email servers, particularly those of the Joint Chiefs, had been compromised. It is significant that the Pentagon said they could not determine how long the email servers had been under the control of the attackers. A later report pegged the cost to recover from the attack at over $100 million.[23]

The air-gapped Secret Internet Protocol Routing Network (SIPRNet) was designed to be completely separate from regular military and civilian networks although it spans the globe and connects many defense contractors, albeit via standalone terminals. Richard Clarke, Former National Coordinator for Security, Infrastructure Protection, and Counter-terrorism for the United States, said in an interview with author Peter Singer: "Why is it that every time a virus pops up on the regular Internet, it also shows up in SIPRNet"? His implication was that, like most networks, there were unaccounted-for connections to the Internet. [24]

The lack of controls within SIPRNet itself was demonstrated in a dramatic fashion when a Universal Serial Bus (USB)-born virus was spread throughout the world after it was introduced in a forward active military operation, probably Afghanistan.[25] Because the infection had such a dramatic impact on the DoD, "a wake up call" according to William Lynn,[26] it is important to look at what was actually a fairly simplistic attack that would have been easily blocked by most organizations.

The malware was identified by the Finnish anti-virus firm F-Secure on June 26, 2008 as worm_w32_agent_btz or Agent.btz for short.[27] It was a variant of a previously seen worm called SillyFDC. "Four months later, in October 2008, NSA analysts discovered the malware on SIPRNet, which the Defense and State departments use to transmit classified material but not the nation's most sensitive information. Agent.btz also infected the Joint Worldwide Intelligence Communication System, which carries top-secret information to U.S. officials throughout the world."[26]

The NSA's Advance Networks Operations (ANO) was the group that discovered Agent.btz in SIPRNet and developed a way to neutralize it. The Joint Task Force-Global Network Operations (JTF-GNO) was responsible for Buckshot Yankee, the clean up effort, while the NSA's Tailored Access Operations (TAO) conducted network surveillance to find variants of Agent.btz.

Buckshot Yankee came with a tremendous cost as 15,000 networks and 7 million PCs in the Department of Defense were scrubbed and re-imaged. It was "the most significant breach of U.S. military computers ever."[26]

A telling interview in 2009 with Lt. Gen. Jeffrey Sorenson, CIO of the army revealed: "In many cases, as we've learned through the most recent Army 'Rampart Yankee' and [Defense Department] 'Buckshot Yankee' exercise — where we had to go off and remediate computer systems because of some infected thumb drives — that was a rather laborious, manually intensive effort to essentially achieve a capability that we would like to have, which would be machine-to-machine."[28] In other words, in 2009 military systems running Windows did not have a mechanism to push software updates effectively, something most organizations have already achieved using Microsoft's System Center Service Manager (SCSM), or third party platforms like those of Lumension or IBM's BigFix.

The DoD's immediate reaction to Buckshot Yankee was to ban the use of USB devices, including thumb drives and CDs, a ban that was not lifted until 2010 while it is still trying to deploy end-point control technology to allow USB thumb drives to be used safely. William Lynn, then Deputy Secretary of Defense for Cyber, claimed that this attack, as late as 2008, was the single most important cause of the Pentagon recognizing the rising threat from cyber attacks and used it to justify standing up the sub-unified Command of US Cyber Command (CYBERCOM). Most military systems now in operational use were designed and specified well before 2008, raising the unanswered question of the cyber hardening incorporated into their design before the military became fully cognizant of the threat.

The DoD Fiscal Year 2011 IT President's Budget Request dated March 9, 2010 states:

> "The AF (Air Force) Network Action Plan is designed to reinvigorate operational rigor and address lingering systemic issues in the AF Global Information Grid highlighted by the Operation BUCKSHOT YANKEE."[29]

By 2013 the military had yet to find a solution to the USB problem and had granted thousands of exceptions to system administrators who need to use thumb drives to maintain computers.[30] This is a problem that was highlighted when both Private Bradley Manning and Edward Snowden used USB devices to steal secret documents. Technologies for endpoint control are widely deployed at many commercial enterprises and had been available for years before Buckshot Yankee.

The defense and intelligence agencies have demonstrated over and over that they have been lulled into a sense of security based on false trust in their systems of protocol and discipline. Army Private Bradley Manning, who was deployed to Iraq and working from a sensitive compartmented information facility, or SCIF, systematically offloaded 251,287 dispatches of secret State Department cables from SIPRNet. He copied them to a CD affixed with a Lady Gaga label and eventually released them to Wikileaks, the biggest leak of secret information up to that time. Most organizations with critical data had long since learned to control such mass copying with technology that alerts when employees exhibit abnormal behavior or copy large amounts of data to a CD, DVD, or USB drive.[31]

The NSA suffered its own massive loss of secret data when contractor Edward Snowden at Booz Allen Hamilton, based in its Hawaii office, downloaded tens of thousands of secret documents and leaked them to journalists at *The Guardian, Der Spiegel, The Washington Post* and other news outlets. After the leak became public in June of 2013, NSA head General Keith Alexander claimed to be making changes to operational security within the 30,000 employee NSA, including reducing the number of system administrators (Snowden's role) and requiring two people to authenticate for access to critical documents.[32] A 2013 revision of security controls in an organization that is on the forefront of cyber offensive operations (as made evident by the content of leaked Snowden documents) has caused considerable consternation within Congress, which has asked the NSA "about who, beyond Mr. Snowden himself, would be held accountable for the security lapses that led to his disclosures."[33]

The late 2013 attack against the Navy Marine Corp Internet (NMCI), purportedly from Iran, bears the hallmarks of an Advanced Persistent Threat (APT). The compromise of the network used by both services for email and communications led to the network being taken down for two days for security upgrades, yet months later there were still signs that the intrusion had not been fully eradicated. Confirmation hearings for Vice Adm. Michael Rogers to be the next head of the NSA were expected to inquire into the four-month cleanup, known as Operation Rolling Tide, overseen by Adm. Rogers as the Navy's chief of cybersecurity.[34]

Examining the documents published by the military and military scholars reveals the absence of concern for future cyber attacks against networked war fighting capabilities. The 300-page monograph on *Command and Control in the Information Age*, written in 2003 by Alberts and Hayes only refers parenthetically to the risk from cyber attacks on command facilities far removed from the theatre of war.[35] A 60 page DARPA Broad Agency Announcement for Communications in Contested Environments dated December 20, 2013 only referred to communications security in passing three times and none of the requested program submissions dealt primarily with security.[36]

The 2014 Quadrennial Defense Review (QDR) makes no mention of software assurance (SA), the practice that Microsoft instituted in 2003 to ensure that software was not rife with buffer overflow or other vulnerabilities.[37]

So it is no wonder that military organizations, the US DoD in particular, are blind to the danger of military cyber attacks. In the following chapters we will track this cyber myopia and we will discover that there are plenty of factors that will be looked back on in future decades as clear indicators that military systems were completely vulnerable, had been designed without a thought for the cyber domain, were eminently exploitable by knowledgeable and capable adversaries, and that a Cyber Pearl Harbor was avoidable.

CHAPTER FOUR

Technology Proceeds War

There is a great debate within academic circles over which comes first: new technology or new types of warfare? Did Hitler's general staff envision mass movement of armored columns before commanding the construction of a mechanized army? Or was it a natural evolution from horseless carriage to armored vehicle? Did King Edward III command the development of the long bow so he could have a victory at Crecy? Or did the long bow evolve until it could make a decisive contribution to warfare? Was gunpowder developed for its celebratory effects or for its lethal characteristics first? Was the telegraph developed to wage war or to revolutionize commercial communication? It certainly had an impact on command and control during the American Civil War with the executive branch supplying daily directions to Lincoln's generals. Likewise, the development of wireless radio drove dramatic changes to warfare as pilots and forward ranging-stations were allowed to communicate.

Nuclear weapons were an offshoot of a revolution in physics. If it were not for the urgency of racing to develop the newfound ability to release energy in unprecedented amounts before the enemy did, perhaps nuclear weapons would not have been developed when they were. They are also a rare example of a weapons system that was developed but never used after the first two such devices were dropped on civilian targets in Japan. Despite the non-use, there is no question that the threat of nuclear weapons has shaped history and the interaction of great powers since their invention.

In a protracted war both sides evolve technology rapidly as an existential threat goads them to innovate, adopt, and invest. The remarkable advances made by the United States during World War II were in part fueled by the mother load of inventions provided by Henry Tizard's British Technical and Scientific Mission. A small team packed a metal box full of documents detailing the scientific secrets Britain had been working on that might have military applications. The onset of the war had stripped Britain of the resources to continue developing them, but the US, not yet engaged, set to work to develop technology for jet engines, and most importantly developed the Magnetron 10 into the game changing radar systems that would turn the tide of battle in the Atlantic.

In the cyber realm there is a similar question, one that is easier to answer because the narrative is so repetitive: Is cyberwar going to evolve from the technology or will the technology shape future wars? Which came first, cyber weapons or their use in war fighting?

Since it is evident that cyber weapons development has progressed dramatically in the last decade and a half and their use in waging war has been very limited to date, it is the case that technology is driving war fighting once again. Just as the long bow was developed for hunting but repurposed to fighting men in armor, gunpowder led to the development of rockets and guns, the internal combustion engine led to mechanized warfare, and wireless communications have changed war fighting irrevocably, so too will the advent of network and computer attacks change future wars.

Cybersecurity is always an afterthought

One of the primary tenets of this book is that security measures are rarely built into new technology. It is not the purpose of this book to find fault with this strategy as it is unavoidable and in fact there is no finger pointing needed. That said, it is valuable to support this contention with its history so that we can understand how we got to where we are and what the future holds.

It is important to remember that as computers evolved they were designed as stand-alone computing machines. Operators would feed data in via a progression of measures. The evolution of technology to feed theses machines spanned toggle switches, paper tape, punch cards, and magnetic tape. Who would want to attack such a machine? They were physically remote and did not even contain data repositories in their first incarnations. It was only later, when the machines could access mass storage, that they became repositories of potentially valuable information. The value in computers that was worth stealing was their ability to compute. Since they were extremely expensive to build and maintain they were only accessible to the largest businesses and government agencies and research labs. The value in a computer became measured in compute cycles that translated into machine time.

Early attacks against computers involved the theft of machine time, so early defenses were essentially protections to account for the machine time of those that accessed the mainframes of the day. These access controls served to restrict access to legitimate account holders and account for their use. In the era of the mainframe, roughly 1960-1980, access control programs like CA's Top Secret and IBM's Resource Access Control Facility (RACF) defined computer security. Malware of the day was limited to runtime programs that would mimic a login screen. The unwary user would sit down at a terminal in a college computer lab or elsewhere and enter his username and password. The attacker would log that information while the user would be passed off to the machine interface, none the wiser until he checked his account to learn their allotted machine time had been depleted.

It did not take long for remote terminals to be hooked up to mainframes allowing schools and researchers to access the power of a computer from afar. Clifford Stoll an astrophysicist and computer administrator at Berkeley Labs, discovered if not the first case of remote access theft, at least the most well publicized. His book, *Cuckoo's Egg*, describes how the discovery of a small discrepancy in the accounting logs of his computer lab led him on a chase around the world. He eventually tracked the hackers (coming in over the extremely slow modems of that time) to Germany where Soviet-backed agents were looking to grab military secrets and pass them off to their masters. Even today many security researchers credit Clifford Stoll's enthralling story with inspiring their careers.

The development of the personal computer in the '70s and '80s led to a new phenomenon: computer viruses widely spread through the sharing of floppy disks. Before networking, all data and software programs had to be distributed through physical means—thin plastic disks covered with a magnetic medium that could store the ones and zeros of computer language. These floppy disks were an evolution and miniaturization of the larger hard disk drives used to store static files attached to a computer.

The motivation for the creators of the early viruses, while malicious in effect, were merely to have fun at the expense of computer users. They took advantage of the lack of security of early PCs to display messages, crash the systems, or erase data.

It did not take long for central services to evolve that mimicked the mainframe-terminal duality for owners of consumer PCs. Bulletin Board Services (BBS) arose to share central resources, allow users to chat with each other, and get access to popular games and programs. Access was through dial-up modems first at 300 bytes per second (1,000 bits/second is 1 kilobaud) then 15, 28, and 56K baud. These early BBSs were the precursor to the Internet. They were islands of connectivity accessed through a telephone number. Services offered included gaming and elaborate chat rooms. And, of course, clever users began to exploit these systems to gain advantage in games or even to take over the operation of the BBS. The TearDrop attack was one means of crashing, rebooting or even taking over control of a BBS. The attacker would gain the ability to kick others off the service, steal their login credentials and in general cause mischief.

While the nascent community of online users was growing, the universities were beginning to build a network of networks: the Internet. A grant from the Defense Advanced Research Projects Agency (DARPA) awarded to contractor BBN created the protocols of the Internet: Transmission Control Protocol and Internet Protocol (TCP/IP). The University of Michigan in Ann Arbor devised the first network router that was deployed to several universities and later connected to ARPA-Net. By 1987 the Michigan network (Merit) along with IBM and MCI won a National Science Foundation contract to build NSFNet which by 1995 become the Internet as commercial entities took over. As more and more nodes were added to the network the value of the network increased. Metcalfe's Law of the value of a network states that it increases with the square of the number of nodes.[1]

Throughout all of this early development of the Internet, security was not much of a concern. That changed when William

Tappen Morris, a student at Corning University, released the first network born worm, the Morris Worm, from a lab at MIT. Morris created a piece of software that would scan for vulnerable nodes on the early network, install itself remotely, and then proceed to scan for more vulnerable nodes to infect. It spread to most of the 2,000 machines connected to the network. The network traffic generated by the worm overwhelmed the network and effectively shut it down.

Note what is a repeated theme in the history of the development of the Internet: first the technology is developed, then the attack, and then the defense.

The first widely deployed security technology was anti-virus software. AV researchers look at samples of each virus and determine what part of it uniquely identifies it. This is the virus-signature. AV software companies grew with the industry. Along with the Internet came email and viruses could be spread faster and more widely now that they did not rely on transfer through the medium of floppy disks. New capabilities were bundled in and many more signatures added until today, 2015, when there are over 50 million viruses with known signatures.

As the Internet became a valuable resource for businesses both for email and access to information the need arose to limit connections with firewalls. There were two directions to early firewall development. The first, represented by TIS Gauntlet and Borderware, were proxy firewalls. For each Internet service (or protocol, such HTTP for web, and FTP for file transfer), a proxy firewall would accept the connection, look up what to do with the request in a policy table, and then reconstitute the request for forwarding to the destination. Proxy firewalls were inherently secure against many unknown attacks because the proxy would not recognize the attack. It was only capable of formulating network requests that complied with the standard for the particular protocol.

The first commercial success in the firewall space, FW-1, was created by a small company in Israel, Check Point Software. FW-1 used a shortcut that made it possible to handle many more connections than a proxy firewall. So-called stateful inspection only looked at packet headers and looked at the ports, sources, and destinations in a stream of TCP/IP packets. It would apply a simple policy of Allow or Deny and the option to Log. At first FW-1 was sold as software to be run on off-the-shelf servers such as Sun Microsystems, HP, IBM, or Silicon Graphics appliances. As the need for higher speeds and number of connections rose, stateful inspection firewalls began to be bundled on specialized hardware. The Wheel Group had one of the first of these. They were acquired by networking giant Cisco and its PIX firewall became the market share leader.

Of the many examples of technology being deployed without an eye towards security, Microsoft Windows was one of the leading examples.

Much thought has gone into what is required for a secure operating system (OS). Strict control of user access and a least-privilege methodology are paramount. In other words, an ordinary user should not be able to commandeer system resources that can impact other users or modify other software. The early versions of Windows had none of these. On top of that, in the rush to add features and push out innovations, Microsoft did very little code review to see if vulnerabilities were being introduced. This story is a prime example of security being layered in as an afterthought.

If Windows had been designed from the beginning with security in mind, much of the course of history would have been changed. The multi-billion dollar industry of AV vendors would have never come about. Worms, viruses, spyware, and cybercrime would never have risen to further fuel the IT security industry.

Security researchers and hackers would eagerly investigate every new release of Windows to be the first to discover new vulnerabilities. On the one hand the researchers would gain bragging rights, and on the other, the hackers would develop new exploits to compromise the millions of home and business computers in use. Because each new version of Windows was built on top of the original, even today vulnerabilities are discovered that existed in Microsoft's very first OS: DOS.

The Windows operating system was the most widely deployed enterprise computing platform in 2001 for desktops and servers, while vulnerabilities were rampant and viruses and worms that exploited those vulnerabilities were growing in number. As later-day evolutions of the Morris Worm and early viruses hammered at Windows machines, a serious look at security was required. Code Red, Nimda, MSBlaster and SQL Slammer[2] provided a wake up call to Microsoft CEO and founder, Bill Gates, who responded with his famous Trustworthy Computing memo[3]. The volume of patches to fix vulnerabilities had grown to such an extent that Microsoft had to switch from a patch release cycle of as-needed to the second Tuesday of every month in order to reduce the operational burden on their customers. Gates' memo set the stage for reeducating all of the programmers at Microsoft in secure software development lifecycle practices. A program of bounties was instituted to encourage researchers to discover and reveal vulnerabilities to Microsoft instead of publishing them or selling them on the emerging market for such intelligence.

In practically every case, new capabilities enabled by the Internet are deployed before adequate protections are added. At launch, new services such as Facebook, Twitter, and Gmail did not have value to attackers. But as they grew and became ubiquitous they became very valuable. The lack of adversaries willing to take advantage of insecure systems allows these new capabilities to grow until they become essential to operations, profits, and market success.[4] Only after they become targets are the requisite security measures added.

Today the battle against new vulnerabilities, and malware that exploits them, is not over but it is under control with the emergence of an IT security industry with over $62 billion in annual spending.[5] In later chapters we will discover how most systems are developed and deployed with little thought to security. These include industrial control systems, medical devices, automobiles, and most importantly for our purposes, Command and Control (C&C), Intelligence, Surveillance, and Reconnaissance (ISR), and weapons platforms; the pillars of Network-Centric Warfighting (NCW).

But first let us examine the rise of NCW from the heyday of the Internet boom.

CHAPTER FIVE

Internet Boom Times

It is hard to capture the excitement of the Internet boom for those who did not experience it directly. It was a new world created by technologists, visionaries, and entrepreneurs. Contemporaneous news reporting was full of superlatives. Warnings of the lawlessness of this Wild West fit the concept of a new frontier—only the mass settling of the American West provided a fitting analogy for what was happening.

The flash point for the Internet boom was the introduction of the first graphical web browser in 1993. Created at the University of Champagne Urbana in Illinois by a young Marc Andreesen, the Mozilla web browser was a simple graphical window onto the World Wide Web. Documents, images, and music were instantly accessible to anyone with an Internet connection. Those connections, usually via dial-up modem, were provided by hundreds of new startup businesses called Internet Service Providers (ISPs). Most of the already thriving BBSs connected their user communities to the Internet, transforming themselves into ISPs. The biggest of these, America On Line, changed the whole social aspect of the Internet when its 3 million customers were granted access. No longer was the Internet the domain of technologists; the introduction AOL brought Grandma and Grandpa to the Internet.

Measures of the enthusiasm for the Internet abound. One such measure was the size of print magazines as their advertising exploded. *The Industry Standard*, a weekly chronicle of the

Internet boom, grew to a thick book of more than 200 pages.[1] To accommodate the growth *The Industry Standard* leased office space throughout San Francisco. To a visitor it appeared that some districts of the capital of Silicon Valley were completely leased by *The Industry Standard*. *Byte Magazine* experienced a similar growth in content and advertising.

Internet startups thrived. Thousands received funding based on little more than an idea for a new web site. Communities, portals, and e-commerce were the hot segments of the day. Even Robert Tappen Morris profited dramatically from one such startup, Viaweb, when he partnered with Paul Graham on a platform that allowed users to build websites. They sold for $49.6 million after only two years of operation.

The Internet boom was felt around the world. In Istanbul they refer to it as the second tulip bubble. (Istanbul, at the crossroads of the Silk Road had experienced an economic boom when trade in tulip bulbs became hyper-inflated.)

Several industry giants of today had their birth in the Internet boom, including Yahoo!, Google, and Amazon. Several startups were funded, grew exponentially, and were acquired for outrageous valuations. Skype, founded by two entrepreneurs in Finland and Estonia, sold for $600 million. HotMail, a free web-based email service, grew and was sold for $2 billion. MySpace, a community/portal, was sold to News Corporation in July 2005 for $580 million (now owned by Specific Media Group and Justin Timberlake, who jointly purchased the company for approximately $35 million in 2011).

Other startups did not fair so well. Pets.com, an e-commerce site for pet supplies, failed dramatically after squandering a $300 million investment.

The enthusiasm for the new digital economy infected the stock market as companies like Paravant Computers, a ruggedized PC manufacturer, Theglobe.com, and Quintus, IPO'd with NASDAQ soaring to all time highs even after Chairman of the Federal Reserve, Alan Greenspan's famously reference to "Irrational Exuberance"

> Clearly, sustained low inflation implies less uncertainty about the future, and lower risk premiums imply higher prices of stocks and other earning assets. We can see that in the inverse relationship exhibited by price/earnings ratios and the rate of inflation in the past. But how do we know when **irrational exuberance** has unduly escalated asset values, which then become subject to unexpected and prolonged contractions as they have in Japan over the past decade?[2]

The enthusiasm for the new digital age was contagious and began to percolate through even the Department of Defense. We will see how Internet era thinking began to be articulated by Arthur Cebrowski in his force transformation efforts. We will also see that Cebrowski and others failed to recognize the rise of cyber threat actors who invariably follow in the path of the cyber frontiersmen.

But first we have to understand the US military thinking of the day. While the Internet was in its infancy the Great Adversary, the Union of Soviet Socialist Republics, was dying.

CHAPTER SIX

First Gulf War

If only the USSR had held on a decade longer, we could have attributed its fall to the Internet. There is still widespread disagreement on the cause of the end of the Cold War between East and West. Was it the war in Afghanistan, the USSR's Viet Nam? Was it the resolve of President Reagan? Was in the enlightenment of Gorbachov? Was it ultimately the success of capitalism over communism? Was it the revolution in communication technology represented by the fax machine? Was it Rock and Roll?

For our story it is important to understand the military posture of both sides just before the final dissolution on December 26, 1991.

As the US, Britain, and the USSR mopped up after WWII the new battle lines of a Cold War were drawn across Eastern Europe. The United States instituted the Marshall Plan to help finance and rebuild Europe. The North Atlantic Treaty Organization (NATO) was constituted to form a coalition bound by a mutual defense treaty to counter the rebuilding of the USSR's military. France, England, and the United States began to build nuclear arms, first with bombs to be delivered by high altitude planes, then with long-range missiles, and finally, Inter-Continental Ballistic Missiles (ICMBs) carried on submarines. This last leg of the nuclear triad provided a surprise attack, or in the worst case a counterattack, capability that put both East and West on a constant footing of readiness for nuclear war.

The primary theater for the expected war between East and West was Europe. Conflicts in Korea and Viet Nam were considered proxy wars, both sides carefully avoiding an escalation that would trigger a massive move by the USSR westward.

During the final phases of the Cold War, Andrew Marshall, head of the US Department of Defense Office of Assessment and Strategic Planning, pushed for a strategy that relied heavily on sensors and information systems to counter Russia's superior ability to amass forces in Europe.[1] From 1976, the US had been moving towards an "offset strategy" that included stealth bombers and fighters and an "assault breaker" strategy that looked to an "intelligence grid" of ISR coupled with communications and precision guided weapons to counter the threatened Soviet incursion into Western Europe.[2] Russian strategists seized on these concepts, calling the move to precision weapons and improvements in sensors and command communications a Military-Technical-Revolution (MTR).

The short and successful 1991 Gulf War, a coalition military action against Iraqi forces in Kuwait that resulted in the complete withdrawal of Iraq in an astoundingly short engagement, caught the attention of military thinkers in Russia and China. On the Russian side, the Gulf War served to validate the MTR: a new shift in war fighting that included better communication, better targeting, and better coordination of fighting forces. Chinese thinking focused on the information warfare aspects. Some of the first papers on what would be termed cyberwar were written in the late '90s by Chinese academic military thinkers.[3,4]

Andrew Marshall, a former RAND analyst-turned-military advisor heading up the Office of Net Assessments within the Pentagon and reporting to the Secretary of Defense, used a broader term than the Russian scholars he studied. He called it a

Revolution in Military Affairs (RMA.) To Marshall, a much more important revolution was occurring. He likened it to the changes that occurred after WWI that led to the inventions of Blitzkrieg, submarine warfare, and air warfare. Marshall favored RMA over MTR because there were much more than technical changes occurring. Changes to organizational structure, hierarchies, and force deployments could be included in the "Revolution."

Marshall defines an RMA as a major change brought about by new technologies combined with a dramatic change in doctrine and organizations.[5] Andrew Krepinevich, a defense policy strategist, extends that definition with the implications for order-of-magnitude increases "in the combat potential and military effectiveness of armed forces."[6]

The volume of writing on RMA reached a peak in 2001 and has tailed off since the terrorist attacks of September 11, 2001.[7] Revolutions in interstate war fighting capabilities paled in comparison to the new thinking required in the face of asymmetric threats represented by a global terrorist organization: Al Qaeda and its many affiliates. Writing on counterinsurgency (COIN) has pushed aside the debate on RMA.[8] Yet that did not stop the momentum in changes to weapons platforms, Command&Control, and organization, that Marshall had set in motion.

In the next chapter we will see how the timing of this new RMA fit nicely with new theories of war fighting as articulated by Arthur Cebrowski.

CHAPTER SEVEN

Cebrowski Force Transformation

Marshall set the stage for a new over-arching strategy of war fighting that encompassed better ISR, coupled with an information grid, and better Command and Control, tied to a communication grid, along with smarter weapons that could be guided to their targets with precision and assurance. This theory of RMA preceded the Internet boom by only a couple of years.

Arthur Cebrowski, appointed director of the Office of Force Transformation by Donald Rumsfeld in 2001, was the chief proponent of something called Network-Centric Warfare (NCW.) His 1998 paper, *Network-Centric Warfare: Its Origin and Future Proceedings*, written while he was still Director for Space, Information Warfare, and Command and Control, is imbued with the excitement of the halcyon days of the Internet boom. Writing in 1998 he stated: "We are in the midst of a revolution in military affairs (RMA) unlike any seen since the Napoleonic Age, when France transformed warfare with the concept of *levée en masse*. Chief of Naval Operations Admiral Jay Johnson has called it 'a fundamental shift from what we call platform-centric warfare to something we call network-centric warfare', and it will prove to be the most important RMA in the past 200 years."[1]

Cebrowski extends the metaphor of the shift from platform-centric computing (mainframes and stand alone mini-computers) to network-centric computing. "This shift is most obvious in the explosive growth of the internet, intranets, and extranets."[2]

In 1998, Cebrowski argued for a transformation in the military that would have the same benefits to operations that network-centric computing had on the US economy. He said it would lead to improved "speed to command" that would achieve the massing of effects instead of the massing of forces. He also called for a shift to bottom-up force organization or "self-synchronization." He uses the shift to a sensor grid backed by a force grid to support his arguments—a concept of networked ISR informing precision targeting and decentralized C2.

Imagine a modern combat soldier who is linked laterally to his patrol and vertically to his commander with instantaneous communication. Couple that with a sensor grid that exposes the enemy forces as well as all of the friendly forces fighting in a conflict zone. This is the vision that Cebrowski had for eliminating the "fog of war" that had plagued every battle since before Roman times. No more flailing about in the byways of rural Virginia trying to find the Army of the Potomac. No more successful feints on the part of the enemy.

It was not unusual for the time (1998) to completely disregard the vulnerabilities and attack vectors made possible by the shift from platform-centric computing to network-centric computing. While the Internet had experienced its share of worms and viruses by then,[3] the true nature of network-based attacks had yet to arise. Code Red, and Nimda had yet to be experienced. The near collapse of the Internet due to SQLSlammer in January 2003 was not on the horizon. Widespread cybercrime, cyber espionage, and Distributed Denial of Service Attacks were yet to mature.

As is so often the case, networking and widespread use of technology were adopted for their immediate benefits while the necessary defenses against future attacks were ignored.

The 1995 Taiwan Straits crisis and its quick resolution are cited by Cebrowski: "Admiral Clemins was able to use e-mail, a very graphic-rich environment, and video teleconferencing to achieve the effect he wanted", which was to deploy the carrier battle groups in a matter of hours instead of days.[4]

The very mention of email for coordinating command and control should raise questions of confidentiality, integrity, and availability, a perspective that Cebrowski lacked. While there is criticism that NCW alone is not the transformative power that Cebrowski foresaw, as the fog of war was still evident in the Iraq War,[5] the continuing development of sensors, precision weapons systems, improved command and control and the dawning awareness of the impact of 'cyber' (as the military began to call networks and computers) on future war fighting, all contribute to an ongoing RMA whose beginnings were in the concepts heralded by Cebrowski.[6]

In a Pentagon briefing to the press shortly after becoming director of the Office of Force Transformation, Cebrowski said, "Network-Centric Warfare should be the cornerstone of transformation." He went on to assert "If you are not interoperable you are not on the net. You are not benefiting from the information age." As will be evident, these words foretold a transformation of military infrastructure to be interoperable, networked, and that strives to see through the fog of war.[7]

In a panel discussion before the American Institute of Aeronautics and Astronautics (AIAA) in 2002, Lt. General Bruce Carlson hailed "a new theory of war based on information age principles and phenomenon," while Lt. General William Tangney, Deputy Commander in Chief of US Special Operations Command at the time, stated, "The key to success in Afghanistan, which we did not have in the Kosovo campaign, was the marriage between the operator on the ground and the aircraft, which allows you to get the precision and targeting."[8]

This was an indication that Cebrowski, who was also on the panel, was seeing his vision fulfilled. Tangney went on to extol the power of putting Hellfire heat-seeking air-to-ground missiles on Predator drones and "creating a data stream" to the ground and marrying that to Global Hawk (the high altitude unmanned ISR platform slated to replace the U2 spy plane[9]) so "you have a capability that you never had before."[10] He also cited the need for Blue Force (friendly forces) tracking, eliminating the fog of war, which would have prevented the three occurrences of fratricide up to that point in Afghanistan. He envisioned weapons systems that would not target locations of friendly forces (very smart bombs). They would incorporate a lock-out mechanism so that friendly forces could not be fired upon. Brookings senior fellow Peter Singer touches on the risk associated with this move toward Blue Force identity when he suggests that an attacker could seek to trick targeting systems into mis-identifying Blue Force components for Red Force.[11] Ralph Peters foretells "battles of conviction" where opposing sides seek to take advantage of vulnerabilities in weapons systems to cause misconfigurations.[12]

Stephen Biddle at the US Army War College Strategic Studies Institute refutes the enthusiasm of Tangney, pointing out that the Taliban fighters quickly adapted to the threat posed by precision laser targeting of exposed positions and began to hide from overhead satellites as well as use ground cover to avoid detection until they fired on US forces.[13]

This vision of networked platforms continues to pervade military thinking. In February, 2015 the Chief of Naval Operations (CNO) Adm. Jonathan Greenert, described plans for a sixth generation Naval carrier-launched fighter jet, the F/A-XX. A press account reads in part:

"One analyst said if Navy F/A-XX developers seek to engineer a sixth-generation aircraft, they will likely explore a range of next-generation technologies such as maximum sensor connectivity, super cruise ability and an aircraft with electronically configured "smart skins."
Maximum connectivity would mean massively increased communications and sensor technology such as having an ability to achieve real-time connectivity with satellites, other aircraft and anything that could provide relevant battlefield information, said Richard Aboulafia, vice-president of analysis at the Teal Group, a Virginia-based consultancy.

And to top it off the CNO suggested: ""The weight that we put on an aircraft due to the pilot is kind of extraordinary. You can take that off and put sensors on there instead," Greenert explained in suggesting that the new fighter could be unmanned.[14]
We will discuss the problems introduced by "massive connectivity" and keeping communications immune to interception and disruption in a later chapter, but for now let's move on to the creation of the DoD's US Cyber Command.

CHAPTER EIGHT

The Rise of CYBERCOM

The lineage of Cyber Command can be traced to the rapid realization, on the part of the military, that the move to NCW had exposed them to network attack (but not to systems level attacks). After witnessing network-based attacks such as Moonlight Maze and after one of the first red team exercises, ELIGIBLE RECEIVER, uncovered vulnerabilities, came the creation of a small Joint Task Force-Computer Network Defense (JTF-CND), which worked with the Defense Information Services Agency (DISA) to provide network security operations. The JTF-CND became operational on 1 December 1998.[1]Under the 1999 Unified Command Plan, JTF-CND was moved from reporting directly to the Secretary of Defense to become part of US Space Command (SPACECOM).[2]

JTF-CND was reorganized as the Joint Task Force-Computer Network Operations (JTF-CNO) in April 2001 after SPACECOM took over DoD's computer network attack planning. Both network defense and attack were thus overseen by the same organization. When SPACECOM was merged into US Strategic Command (STRATCOM) in 2002, JTF-CNO had just 122 personnel.

In 2004 Secretary Rumsfeld assigned the three-star general in charge of DISA to have the additional role of heading up the JTF-Global Network Operations within STRATCOM, an extension and raising-up of JTF-CNO. And finally in 2005, as STRATCOM was broken into several functional commands, the Joint Functional Component Command for Network Warfare (JFCC-NW) was assigned to the Director of the NSA. This meant that network operations (JTF-CNO) was paired with DISA and network intelligence and security (JFCC-NW) was assigned to the NSA.

Meanwhile, each of the services was scrambling to lead the way in offensive and defensive cyber by extending their own capabilities. After the Joint Chiefs of Staff declared that the Armed Forces must have the ability to operate across the air, land, sea, space, and cyberspace domains of the battlespace,"[3], the Air Force established the Operational Command for Cyberspace in June, 2006.[4] By November, they had provisionally announced the creation of the Air Force Cyber Command (AFCYBER), but by 2008, the Air Force had backed away from trying to lead in cyberspace and assigned cyber operations to a new numbered wing, the 24th Air Force.[5] The Navy created the US Navy Fleet Cyber Command/10th Fleet in January 2010 as part of the joint functional command of USCYBERCOM.[6]

To attempt to cut through the confusion, Secretary of Defense Gates created a review process and after some deliberation called for the creation of a sub-unified Command under a four-star general under USSTRATCOM which "should be DoD's organizational end state for cyber" Command and Control.[7]

Lieutenant General Keith Alexander, who commanded both the NSA and JFCC-NW, was given the additional command of JTF-GNO in November of 2008, putting both the offensive and defensive components of cyberwar in close contact with the intelligence gathering function of the NSA. This decision, according to CIA historian Michael Warner, assigned to US Cybercom, was made in part because of the NSA's key role in identifying and eradicating the Agent.btz worm from defense networks.[8]

On June 23, 2009 Gates directed STRATCOM to abolish

JFCC-NW and JTF-GNO and form a new unified command designated as US Cyber Command (USCYBERCOM). Personnel from the disbanded units would move to USCYBERCOM. By May 21, 2010 Alexander was promoted to a four-star general and USCYBERCOM had achieved Initial Operational Capability.[9] On October 31, 2010, USCYBERCOM was deemed to be at Full Operational Capability (FOC) by Deputy Secretary William J. Lynn III.

According to its fact sheet, USCYBERCOM is a sub-unified command subordinate to U.S. Strategic Command (USSTRATCOM). Service Elements include Army Forces Cyber Command (ARFORCYBER), 24th USAF, Fleet Cyber Command (FLTCYBERCOM), and Marine Forces Cyber Command (MARFORCYBER).[10] The creation of USCYBERCOM took place over a remarkably short period of time (from 2008-2010) as the DoD began to recognize the importance of offensive cyber. It is only since 2013 and the Snowden revelations that we have learned that the NSA had been developing tremendous capabilities in Computer Network Attack and Exploitation (CNA and CNE), even prior to the creation of USCYBERCOM.

By tracing the early history of USCYBERCOM it is possible to understand some of the reasons why the military has focused almost completely on network defense and cyber attack while being unaware of the need to address the vulnerabilities in systems that could be exploited in future conflicts against technologically capable adversaries. It is a problem mirrored in most organizations. The network security staff are separate from the endpoint security staff who manage desktops through patch and vulnerability management tools and ensure that software and anti-virus signatures are up to date. Meanwhile, the development teams that create new applications, web services, and digital business ventures, work completely on their own with little concern for security. The analogous behavior observed in the military is the creation of new weapons systems, ISR platforms, precision targeting, and C2 capabilities without ensuring that they are resistant to the types of attacks that USCYBERCOM and the NSA have been researching and deploying.

USCYBERCOM had its genesis in NCW thinking. First the military worked to participate in the information revolution by joining their networks together. Then it recognized the need for protecting those networks, now deemed cyberspace. The concept that a strong defense requires a strong offense, carried over from missile defense and Cold War strategies, led to a focus on network attack and less emphasis on improving resiliency of computing platforms and weapons systems.

Since its Full Operational Capability, USCYBERCOM has continued to build its force and capability.

USCYBERCOM growth

In March 2013 General Alexander provided details on how USCYBERCOM was being organized to "focus on defending the nation in cyberspace," including the formations of three sets of teams.[11] Thirteen teams would be tasked with defending the nation's infrastructure with offensive cyber means. Twenty-seven teams would coordinate offensive cyber operations with the combatant commands. An unspecified number of teams would be responsible for defending the Department of Defense's own networks. One-third of the teams were slated to be operational by September 2013, one-third by late 2014, and the final third a year later.[12]

By February, 2015 a DoD spokesperson indicated that

completing Alexander's target of a fully staffed mission of 6,000 cyber warriors was slipping. Only 3,000 had been hired:

> Lt. Col. Valerie Henderson, a Pentagon spokeswoman, told Nextgov, "We are about halfway through the overall build, in terms of manning for the cyber mission forces and continue to make progress in training and equipping the teams." She declined to provide a timeline for reaching that size.[13]

NextGov goes on to provide a projected breakdown of how those teams will be deployed:

> "The command comprises three types of 'Cyber Mission Forces' teams:
> About 2,720 will serve on Cyber Protection Teams that safeguard dot-mil systems stateside and abroad.
> Roughly 780 individuals will work within National Mission Teams that repel incoming attacks against key industries, including the health care sector. Some 1,620 will belong to Combat Mission Teams that support overseas warfighters."

In the wake of widespread criticism of the NSA's mass surveillance, the President appointed a review board who recommended that the NSA and USCYBERCOM be split and put under separate commands. On December 13, 2013 the White House announced its decision to preserve the existing arrangement under a single commander and confirmation hearings for Admiral Michael Rogers to replace General Alexander were under way.[14]

"The Army four-star also said in his written statement that in addition to 917 troops and civilians at Cyber Command headquarters in Maryland (with a budget for FY13 of $191 million), there are more than 11,000 people from all four armed services working cyber issues for the command." In addition to those Alexander counts as working with CYBERCOM, Foreign Policy tallied between 53,000 to 58,000 working in cyber from the number claimed by each service.

While CYBERCOM is tasked with defending military networks, in June of 2013 the world learned of the NSA's extensive capability to engage in cyber attacks for the purpose of espionage. The next chapter reveals just some of the capabilities that have come to light since the original Snowden revelations.

CHAPTER NINE

NSA Cyber War Footing

The NSA's offensive cyber capability

The National Security Agency (NSA), led by Gen. Keith Alexander, USCYBERCOM's first commander(now retired), has proven to be very good at offensive cyber.

Revelations from documents stolen from the NSA by contractor Edward Snowden have demonstrated two things: lack of adequate internal security, and comprehensive capabilities to penetrate systems and collect data.

The NSA, even with its vast resources and funding, ($10.8 billion according to leaked documents[1] neglected its own internal operational security to an extent that allowed a low-level system administrator to abscond with tens of thousands of classified documents. According to a tally kept by leak site cryptome.org, 4,197 pages of 58,000 files that *The Guardian* first reported, have been published as of June 4, 2015.[2] This is just one more example of the military's vulnerability to an adversary who gains access to its internal system, easy for an insider like Manning or Snowden, or by implication, a foreign agent or mole with access to their networks. This lack of effective operational security pales in comparison to the methodologies developed by Lockheed Martin over a decade of building a defense against so called Advanced Persistent Threats (APTs).

Through its Security Intelligence Center (SIC), Lockheed

Martin has developed a Cyber Kill Chain[3] methodology to counter targeted attacks, a technique that successfully stopped the hackers who managed to steal the seeds to RSA SecurID tokens and use them to attempt to get into Lockheed Martin's networks in 2011. The Cyber Kill Chain methodology involves continuous network packet capture and analysis. That analysis includes data mining for key indicators of compromise (IoC) and "detonating" malware samples to observe their behavior. The Cyber Kill Chain is their classification of the stages of an advanced attack: reconnaissance, weaponization, delivery, exploitation, installation, C2, and actions on objectives. Each stage requires different tools to detect, deny, disrupt, degrade, deceive, and destroy an adversary's attempt to intrude on a network. It was not until security company Mandiant released its impactful APT1 report [4] that the industry began to provide commercial tools to operationalize the type of activities that Lockheed Martin's SIC engages in around the clock. From the questions raised about Snowden's actions it is evident that the NSA trusted doctrine alone to prevent system administrators from abusing their access. In the wake of the Snowden affair, General Keith Alexander described plans to deploy technology to reduce the number of system admins and require two people to authenticate to engage in their system maintenance duties. Alexander said, "What we're in the process of doing—not fast enough—is reducing our system administrators by about 90 percent," or from 1,000 to about 100.[5]

The second lesson to be learned from the content of Snowden's documents released to date is that the NSA has built a global capability to execute on a plan of information dominance for intelligence gathering, a term used somewhat differently in the RMA literature where 'information dominance" implies complete battle space situational awareness, not the universal collection of

SIGINT from the internet and cell phone providers.

Ostensibly to collect enough communications meta data and content to deter, disrupt, and destroy terrorists and their plans, the NSA's capabilities have also been used for broader spying on foreign leaders, and through its partner agencies within the UK, Canada and Australia, intercept communications that appear to have an economic motivation.[6]

An examination of the capabilities that the NSA has developed and deployed provides a window into advanced cyber attack methods. Based on the sophistication of these methods and the tools that the NSA has operationalized, it is possible to question whether the rest of the defense community is capable of defending against these types of advanced attacks. Famed cryptography expert Bruce Schneier has warned that the tools and techniques revealed in the Snowden documents will be used in the near future by cyber criminals and adversary nations.[7]

The catalogue of capabilities revealed in a detailed listing of the Tailored Access Operations (TAO) group based in Texas is an indicator of what offensive cyber operations look like. What is lacking so far is any acknowledgement that US weapons systems, targeting, ISR, and C2 communications should be evaluated, let alone hardened against such attacks.

The NSA has developed the global capacity to intercept data as it travels across Internet backbones and the ability to mine tremendous amounts of captured data in near real time.

XKEYSCORE is one such data mining tool. The capability to select targets and the types of data to extract from the stream is demonstrated by the ability to detect and capture when a Windows PC crashes and the crash report, which contains data from memory that reveals machine settings and even account passwords, is stored in the NSA's data centers.[8]

The data from particular targets on the Internet or from cell phone calls are extracted too. Another capability is to capture location data from cell phone calls that are also carried across the undersea cables that the NSA and GCHQ monitor. Data sent from commonly deployed applications, notably popular game Angry Birds, is also captured.[9]

Quantum and FoxAcid, as described by the leaked documents, are effective means of attack. FoxAcid servers are strategically placed on Internet backbones. They can deliver multiple exploits against someone browsing the web. Via the Quantum Injection program, once a target is identified packets are injected into the download of web pages that direct the browser to receive the exploit code from the FoxAcid server.[10]

Other documents, apparently not provide by Snowden, as reported in *Der Spiegel*, go on to reveal a catalogue of capabilities that TAO has developed through a special team referred to only as ANT.[11]

DEITYBOUNCE is a persistent application attack that exploits the motherboard BIOS of Dell PowerEdge servers. Persistence is the quality of malware to be re-installed after it has been removed. A back door in BIOS indicates that the malware resides well below the operating system, so is undetectable by traditional anti-virus tools.[12]

Through *interdiction*, a term referring to interception of a computer when it is shipped to a target, the IRONCHEF software and hardware back doors are installed. From the catalogue: "If the software CNE implant is removed from the target machine, IRONCHEF is used to access the machine, determine the reason for removal of the software, and then reinstall the software from a listening post to the target system." In other words, the attacker in close proximity can reinstall the software back door after it is removed.[13]

Routers and firewalls from networking vendors Juniper and Cisco are also vulnerable to malware that the NSA can deploy that is difficult to detect and remove, even after their operating systems are re-installed. The Juniper exploit, dubbed FEEDTROUGH, "can, by design, even survive 'across reboots and software upgrades'." This level of persistent threat is reminiscent of the most advanced type of cyber attack emanating from China and documented in security company Mandiant's APT1 report. FEEDTROUGH is the C&C channel that is used to detect software upgrades and reinstall two back doors, DNT's (Digital Network Technology) BANANAGLEE and CES's ZESTYLEAK.[14]

Ironically, the first published case of a back door in Huawei gear is "[t]he HALLUXWATER Persistence Back Door implant" which "is installed on a target Huawei Eudemon firewall as a boot ROM upgrade."[15] Another product, HEADWATER, is a similar back door for Huawei routers.[16] This is ironic because there has been a concerted campaign to limit Chinese manufacturer Huawei from entering US markets and the reason offered is the danger of Chinese back doors in Huawei gear. It has even been shown from Snowden documents that the NSA has penetrated Huawei's own network to install back doors on equipment being shipped to targeted countries in Africa.

The demonstration of interdiction being used against products from Cisco and Juniper, graphically highlighted by an image published in Glenn Greenwald's book of a Cisco shipping box being processed in an NSA site, raises the question: What is being done within the DoD supply chain to ensure that military systems are not being tampered with in a similar fashion?

A localized means of attack against target cell phones is the equipment dubbed TYPHOON HX. This equipment mimics a femto cell access point for cell phone calls and is a method of intercepting voice and data communications when the target is in close proximity.[17] In a battlefield, similar equipment could be deployed on UAVs or ground stations to intercept command and control communications. CANDYGRAM is a simpler device that alerts an operative when a particular handset enters within range.

Remote illumination of embedded devices with radar is an old technique memorialized by George Kennan's experience while he was Ambassador to the Soviet Union. Known as the "Great Seal bug," a radar-illuminated device was planted in the wall behind the Great Seal of the United States above Kennan's desk in the Moscow ambassadorial residence, Spaso House.[18] The KGB was able to bounce radar waves off the device, which would modulate the reflected signal in accord with sound waves it picked up. It was a passive, undetectable bug that could eavesdrop on the conversations in Kennan's office. The TAO catalog has several examples of devices that work on the same principal, but are miniaturized to the point where they can be installed in computer equipment and either provide a passive audio bug or transmit information directly from the host computer. LOUDAUTO is an example of a "room audio" collection device. It measures less than 2 cm across.[19]

Other hardware back doors are illustrated in the TAO catalog. There is a long history of theories about the presence of hardware back doors, especially in Chinese equipment, with Huawei and ZTE being singled out as culprits,[20] yet the TAO catalog is the first public documentation of details of hardware back doors in computer equipment. In addition to the software back doors in Cisco, Juniper, and several hard drive manufacturers, these hardware back doors can be installed in any computer. The additional capability to intercept a computer that has been ordered online by a target of interest and install software or hardware back doors is a microcosm of what supply chain risks exist in all purchases of computer components.

The ANT catalog continues, describing NIGHTSTAND, which is a WiFi injection tool kit that can inject malware into any PC attached to an attacked wireless network.

SOMBERKNAVE is a "Windows XP wireless software implant that provides covert internet connectivity for isolated targets."[21] Delivered over the Internet, it uses the PC's 802.11 WiFi transceiver to connect to any wireless access point and "phone home."

Implants are cataloged for iPhones (DROPOUTJEEP) and GSM SIM cards for mobile phones (GOPHERSET and MONKEYCALENDAR).

Wireless attacks raise the specter of electronic warfare (EW) and questions about weapons platforms and their resilience against such attacks.

This collection of tools revealed in the ANT catalogue are significant in that each one demonstrates the types of sophisticated attacks that can be made against targets. While the Signals Intelligence Directorate (SID) of the NSA, under which TAO operates, targets systems for intelligence collection, these tools are the best examples of the types of tools that would be used in cyberwar against a military that has moved to a NCW footing.

On June 1, 2012 David Sanger exposed the story behind the first documented case of cyber sabotage, Stuxnet, in a front-page story in *The New York Times*. The lead from the story read:

"From his first months in office, President Obama secretly ordered increasingly sophisticated attacks on the computer systems that run Iran's main nuclear enrichment facilities, significantly expanding America's first sustained use of cyberweapons, according to participants in the program."[22]

While the US has yet to admit to Stuxnet formally, journalists at *The Washington Post* and National Public Radio have confirmed that they too have sources that support Sanger's story. [23,24] Snowden also later confirmed in an interview that Stuxnet was co-written by the US and Israel.[25] Stuxnet was part of a secret campaign dubbed Operation Olympic Games. It was preceded by spyware that operatives called "the bug," which mapped the networks and systems inside Natanz, the Iranian uranium refinement facility. Stuxnet was then reportedly delivered via USB thumb drive and over several years did significant damage to the gas centrifuges used to refine uranium. Stuxnet was successful, according to admissions from Iran. Analysts hypothesize that Stuxnet set back Iran's plans to develop nuclear weapons by as much as two years.[26]

Stuxnet is worth studying because its sophistication may well be representative of future attacks deployed against military capabilities: delivery, search and install, compromise, and destruction.

Step 1. Delivery. A secure operation, such as refining uranium for nuclear power and reputedly weapons production, would be walled off from the Internet. Best practices for any critical environment is to ensure that there is no connection to any other network. Internet Protocol networks have to be scanned continuously to ensure that that "air-gap" is not compromised. Network discovery tools are required to ensure that the secure network has not been connected or bridged to the outside world via a rogue WiFi hotspot, satellite link, or trusted third party connection. When a critical network is completely cut off from the rest of the world, there is a tendency to be lax in traditional security operations, as demonstrated in both the cases of Bradley Manning and Edward Snowden. Manufacturers, power plant and electrical power grid operators, and oil and gas transporters, like to think that their systems are air-gapped too.

Every production system needs some way of securely transferring data from the trusted side to the untrusted side and USB thumb drives are often the means for doing so.

The Stuxnet authors recognized that USB tokens were the most viable vector for attacking Iran's nuclear environment. They used a previously unknown vulnerability in Windows software that would automatically execute a program if it was viewed with Windows Explorer.[27] This was similar to the type of vulnerability that the Agent.btz worm used to infect SIPRNet.

Step 2. Search and infect. Once an initial infection was accomplished, probably by an insider or a contractor, the Stuxnet worm would spread to adjacent machines on the network. Unlike APTs that usually report back to a command and control server at this point, Stuxnet had to be autonomous because of that air-gap in the network. Its goal: to find and infect machines running Siemens' Step7 Software. Worms have a tendency to get out of control and if they are not throttled, they can spread to the entire Internet in moments. The 2003 SQLSlammer worm spread to 80,000 machines in less than twelve minutes and caused most of the Internet to screech to a halt.[28] Even Robert Tappan Morris recognized this when he crafted the first Internet worm in 1988. He attempted to avoid a wildfire by only allowing each infection to spread to a few machines before stopping and it still cascaded out of control. Stuxnet used the same throttling. Each infection would only spread to several machines.[29]

Step 3. Compromise via root kit installation. Once Stuxnet was lodged on a PC running Step7, it would replace the dll (dynamic link library) used to communicate with the machine controllers on the plant floor. Step7 is the control software used to communicate new instructions to programable logic controllers (PLCs). Stuxnet would intercept these commands, look for a particular block of data and replace it. If the particular block it was looking for was not detected, it would hand commands off to the original dll, effectively hiding its presence in the many infections that occurred that did not further its mission.

In addition to the "zero-day" vulnerability Stuxnet used for initial infection, it took advantage of three other previously unknown vulnerabilities for privilege escalation, which are required to install software on locked down PCs.[30] The attackers also realized that the operating system would only install software that was digitally signed, so they used stolen digital certificates from Realtek Semiconductor and JMicron Technology to masquerade as a trusted install.[31]

Step 4. Sabotage. Once Stuxnet found its way onto the right machine that controlled the right PLC attached to the right motor control, it modified the instructions sent to that motor causing it to spin at different rates. Machinery rotating at high rotation rates are very sensitive to changes, and gas centrifuges for refinement of radioactive uranium spin at 6,000 RPM. Reports from Iran indicate that their enrichment operations have suffered continuous setbacks since the Stuxnet infection.

Stuxnet is the high-water mark for targeted attacks so far. Yet the methodologies used are not new, even if the result—industrial sabotage–is unprecedented.

Countering a targeted attack on the level of Stuxnet requires a revamping of traditional IT security operations. Examples given in the following chapters indicate that most military systems have not been designed to counter this level of targeting, let alone the combination of destructive intent with the capabilities inherent in the ANT tool kits.

CHAPTER TEN

Assurance

Supply Chain Assurance

The US military has begun to study supply chain vulnerabilities: those parts of the entire specification, design, and acquisition process that could be disrupted by an adversary. One aspect of supply chain management looks at the availability of critical components. Is there a silicon chip, component board, or strategic raw material that could disrupt the ability of a platform to be operationally available if that component were not available? And if so, can alternative sources be found? Another aspect of supply chain management is the elimination of counterfeit parts, a significant problem according to a Congressional report.[1] The aspect that is hardest to address is the existence of back doors in supplied computer components. The ANT tools for installing software back doors in Cisco, Juniper, and Huawei firewalls and routers have not even begun to be addressed by those manufacturers, let alone their customers. Methods of detecting design changes made to silicon are in their infancy and often require destructive testing such as chemically etching the chips. Future supply chain assurance will mean inspecting components for additional features that creep in during the manufacturing or shipping steps. This vulnerability was highlighted in IEEE *Spectrum*:

"A single plane like the DOD's next generation F-35 Joint Strike Fighter, can contain an 'insane number' of chips, says one semiconductor expert familiar with that aircraft's design. Estimates from other sources put the total at several hundred to more than a thousand. And tracing a part back to its source is not always straightforward."[2]

The military has become concerned with the number of integrated circuits that are built overseas and the inability to ensure that the designs have not been tampered with. From DARPA's Microsytems Technology Office:

"The United States does not have a comprehensive program to certify that integrated circuits (ICs) going into U.S. weapons systems do not contain malicious circuits. In response to these concerns, DARPA has initiated its TRUST in Integrated Circuits program to develop technologies that will ensure the trust of ICs used in military systems, but designed and fabricated under untrusted conditions."[3]

The TRUST in IC program is still in its infancy.

Software assurance and the Joint Strike Fighter

The original contracts for the F-35 Joint Strike Fighter were granted in 2001, at a time when the ideals of network-centric warfare of Marshall, Cebrowski, and Owens were most influential. While the joint platform specifications to develop a fighter jet platform that is slower and less maneuverable than its incumbents at the time, and at far greater expense have been criticized, there are indications that the F-35 was specified, designed, and built with little concern for resilience to future cyber attacks.

Reports of program delays because of software issues are revealing in their lack of mention of what has become known as Software Assurance (SA), the practice of software development that seeks to ensure no vulnerabilities are incorporated in the code. This should come as no surprise because the discipline only started to gain maturity in recent years. Microsoft famously put all development on hold in 2002 after Bill Gates issued his Trustworthy Computing memo. What ensued was a year-long effort to train all software developers in secure coding practices. Only after a decade has this resulted in fewer security vulnerabilities in the Windows operating system. Only with Windows 8 has the Trusted Platform Module (TPM), a hardware root of trust, been integrated with Windows.

Software is at the core of all of the technology necessary to realize the vision of network-centric warfare. Command and Control, ISR, logistics, and precision targeting all rely on software. The vision of reducing the fog of war through complete battlefield situational awareness, the identity of friend and foe, terrain and weather mapping, and geo-spacial location relies on software embedded in weapons platforms, vehicles, satellites, drones, and communications systems.

The F-35 Joint Strike Fighter is designed to provide unprecedented situational awareness to the pilot. Data from radar and other sensors is collected real-time, processed against a "data-load" prepared for the specific mission which includes the electronic signatures and radar profiles of known adversary weapons, aircraft, etc. and projects them on a panoramic display or eventually in a helmet mounted display. Instead of a "blip" on a screen the pilot can see an intuitive graphic that lets him know what and where a threat is.

Software assurance practices seek to reduce the theoretical attack surface of a platform or networked system. Training of developers in secure software practices is just one element of software assurance. Tools have been developed to automatically scan source code for vulnerabilities. [HP Fortify, Veracode, IBM

Appscan] The most common things to look for include non-specified memory address allocation whereby a virus or worm can overflow a memory buffer to cause malicious code to be executed, or the lack of validating input values. These vulnerabilities can be introduced at all levels, including the BIOS in a chip, the communication layers within the CPU, the operating system, and the thousands of applications that run on each platform.

Military weapons and communications platforms tend to run on proprietary, custom-built software and even operating systems. This has actually been an advantage over the last decade because these systems are not vulnerable to the common viruses and worms that attack most commercially available systems. Reuse of malware developed by cyber criminals against these systems would not work against the custom-built weapons platforms.

Of course the military's use of Windows platforms in their operational environments has exposed their IT departments to the constant battle against malware that the rest of the world faces, as demonstrated by Buckshot Yankee. As late as January 2015 J. Michael Gilmore, the Director of Operational Test & Evaluation for the DoD, reported that all but one of the networks they evaluated failed to defend against their targeted attacks.[4] Reading between the lines of his office's 440-page annual report it is possible to discern that cyberdefense within the 16 tested Commands is still in its infancy. Those Commands that did well practiced good password controls and reviewed logs. No mention is made of advanced malware defense, sandboxing, or network security analytics, the new tools of cyberdefense.

But weapons systems have mostly avoided these issues because most of them are not built on Windows. Systems that are proprietary have benefited from this "security by obscurity" only because there have not been adversaries who have had the resources to obtain the systems and conduct the research to devise exploits against them. It would take a concerted espionage effort to obtain source code from these systems in development or even compiled code from operational systems. Of course, there have been incidents of code theft and system acquisition.

On April 1, 2001, a Navy EP-3E plane flying over the South China Sea was forced out of the air by an overzealous PLA Navy pilot who bumped his J-8 fighter jet into the spy plane. The Chinese fighter pilot crashed and died. The US plane had been flying a regular ISR mission and contained 24 personnel assigned to the NSA's field operations tasked with intercepting signals from the Chinese mainland. While protocol required the personnel to wipe all hard drives, they did not have time after a forced landing to destroy the on-board computer systems. While the ensuing diplomatic incident, the first of George W. Bush's presidency, was resolved, it only became evident years later that the US had suffered a major intelligence loss. The secret operating system of the NSA had been compromised.

"The Navy's experts didn't believe that China was capable of reverse-engineering the plane's NSA-supplied operating system, estimated at between thirty and fifty million lines of computer code, according to a former senior intelligence official. Mastering it would give China a road map for decrypting the Navy's classified intelligence and operational data."[5]

writing in *The New Yorker,* Seymour Hirsh, went on to describe an unusual incident. China blatantly flooded communication channels known to be monitored by the NSA with decrypted US intercepts, sending the signal that China had been able to leverage the captured intelligence from the Navy spy plane.

"A few weeks after Barack Obama's election [in 2008], the Chinese began flooding a group of communications links known to be monitored by the NSA with a barrage of intercepts," two Bush Administration national-security officials and the former senior intelligence official told Hirsh. The intercepts included details of planned American naval movements. The repercussions were dramatic as the Navy had to re-deploy a hardened operating system throughout their systems at a cost of hundreds of millions of dollars.[5]

In a military steeped in security thinking, the loss of control of a single system that held encryption keys would kick off an immediate rekeying effort. The primary industry protocol for rekeying remote systems, Key Management Interoperability Protocol (KMIP), has yet to be widely deployed anywhere within the US military since its October 1, 2010 official release.[6] Distribution of encryptions keys is handled manually.

Iran and North Korea have both captured US drones. In at least one case Iran has demonstrated that they were able to decrypt stored video data (if it was indeed even encrypted). These are additional examples of platform losses that should kick off a complete rekeying of encryption keys throughout any system that relied on the lost keys, in much the same way that consumers are urged to change their passwords when a breach compromises them.

In the litany of wake-up calls that the US military has experienced, the exfiltration of terabytes of data from the Defense Industrial Base was the single biggest loss of data of weapons systems. Government sources have quantified the loss in terms of number of bytes but not in terms of actual content.

In a PowerPoint slide leaked to *Der Spiegel* the NSA confirms the attack against the Defense Industrial Base (DIB). They attribute the theft to Chinese industrial cyber espionage and gave the incident the code name Byzantine HADES. In addition to stealing 50 terabytes of design data the NSA slides reveal:

-There were over 30,000 incidents of cyber attack, 500 of which were "Significant intrusions in DoD Systems"

-At least 1,600 network computers penetrated

-At least 600,000 user accounts compromised

-Total cost to assess and repair damage was over $100 million

While the focus has been on the repercussions of design data being stolen that could assist China in developing their next stealth capable fighter, they do not indicate that software source code could have been part of the stolen trove. The loss of design data means that eventually US war fighters may have to face advanced capability Chinese fighter jets, but the loss of software has the much more imminent consequence that the F-35 Joint Strike Fighter may suffer from cyber attacks in the next conflict with a technologically advanced adversary.

The F-35 JSF, in its various configurations for the Navy, Marine Corps, and Air Force, has suffered many program delays and cost overruns. This complex system includes stealth technology, helmet-mounted heads-up displays, and even has a short take off and landing configuration for the Marine Corps. A report from management consultants A.T. Kearney titled *Delivering Military Software Affordably* describes the exponential growth in lines of code for military systems over the years. It states:

"The F-35 already has cost the DoD billions of dollars and has surpassed its delivery date by several years. No definite timeline is yet set for when the Navy, the Air Force, or the Marines will receive a fully operational version of the plane. In the meantime, costs continue to rise. The Pentagon recently confirmed the F-35 program's estimated development and sustainment costs are likely to be $1 trillion over the aircraft's 50-year projected life."[7]

There are over nine million lines of custom code for the JSF's onboard systems alone. An additional fifteen million lines of software are still to be rolled out for the logistics system that has been designed to support the aircraft. According to Michael J. Sullivan, Director Acquisition and Sourcing Management for the DoD: "JSF software development is one of the largest and most complex projects in DOD history."[8]

The Air Force recently tested millions of lines of code by scanning them with a software assurance tool. The results from the test were telling. They found one software vulnerability per 8 lines of code, one "high vulnerability" per 31 lines of code and one "critical vulnerability" per seventy lines of source code.[9] Based on these numbers the onboard software on the F-35 could contain over 128,000 critical vulnerabilities, any one of which could be exploited to reduce the fighter's effectiveness or in the worst case be used to disable its fire control, re-direct it in flight, cut off communications, or disable it completely. Assuming that an adversary does not have such a capability is dangerous in the extreme, especially after learning from the compromise of systems derived from the captured EP-E3 ISR platform.

A report created by Cigital, a company that produces secure software development lifecycle frameworks, concluded in part: "Today's software is riddled with both design flaws and implementation bugs, resulting in an unacceptable security risk. In our experience, the need for software security is underscored by the increasing number of vulnerabilities in production systems with Authority To Operate (ATO)."[10]

The concepts of software assurance and secure software development life cycles are new relative to most weapons systems deployed over the last decade. The story of Microsoft's radical shift to a secure SDL provides a measure of the type of effort that is required: an effort to change a culture within a large organization. According to Microsoft's own history,[11] the damage their products and their reputation received from multiple worms, CodeRed, Nimda, SQLSlammer, and MSBlaster, led to the call-to-arms email from their founder, Bill Gates, the Trustworthy Computing Memo. In his missive, dated January 11, 2002, Gates said:

"Computing is already an important part of many people's lives. Within ten years, it will be an integral and indispensable part of almost everything we do. Microsoft and the computer industry will only succeed in that world if CIOs, consumers and everyone else sees that Microsoft has created a platform for Trustworthy Computing."[12]

Gates' memos to Microsoft employees usually marked successful shifts in his company's strategy. The May 1995 "Internet Tidal Wave" memo, was a call to action to network Windows computers. Its enthusiasm was reflected by Cebrowski and Owens, describing their visions of network-centric warfare only a few years later. The Trustworthy Computing memo led to Microsoft halting all software development in February 2002 while they trained over 9,000 developers in the methods of secure SDL. Even with that unprecedented action, Microsoft code continues to have severe vulnerabilities to this day,[13] which demonstrates the magnitude of the task.

William Lynn's *Foreign Affair* article is often cited as the DoD's 'wake up call' memo, [14]yet there is little evidence that the concept of a secure SDL has penetrated the culture of defense system specification and acquisition. The National Institute for

Standards and Testing (NIST) responsible for creating most Feneral cybersecurity guidelines   only published a guide to *Security Considerations in the System Development Life Cycle* in October 2008, in which software vulnerabilities are treated as paramount concerns.[15]

The Joint Strike Fighter is only one of many instances of US weapons systems being targeted by Chinese cyber spies. In the next chapter we look for other signs that weapons systems are vulnerable.

CHAPTER ELEVEN

Military Cyber Failure

Just as with commercial enterprises there is a long history of successful compromise of IT systems within the US military. And just as with banks, retail outlets, and manufacturing, it is only after a successful breach or disruption that steps are taken to prevent future occurrences.

In December 2009 it was learned that the CIA had recovered laptops in Iraq and Afghanistan with hundreds of hours of video streams from American surveillance drones. *The Wall Street Journal* reported, "Shiite fighters in Iraq used software programs such as SkyGrabber -- available for as little as $25.95 on the Internet -- to regularly capture drone video feeds...." Evidently the US knew of this lack of encryption of video feeds from ISR systems since the 1990s but had relied on the lack of technical sophistication of its insurgent adversaries. "The U.S. government has known about the flaw since the U.S. campaign in Bosnia in the 1990s, current and former officials said. But the Pentagon assumed local adversaries wouldn't know how to exploit it, the officials said." *The Wall Street Journal* then went on to quote sources that indicated the drone platforms were ten-year-old technology and built on proprietary systems that were not able to incorporate standard encryption libraries. Encrypting links would have added to the program costs.[1]

In December 2011 a Lockheed RQ-170 stealth drone was apparently diverted from its mission over Iran and landed near Kashmar inside Iran. Iran claimed that their cyber military unit had jammed command and control to the drone and spoofed GPS signals to trick it into landing locally. Dan Goure, an analyst at the Lexington Institute in Arlington, VA. opined that the normal operation of the drone should have at least sent it back to base if it lost its command and control connection.[2]

In February 2013 Iran released footage purportedly taken from the drone's video camera of it landing in Kandahar, one of the bases for US drone operations into Pakistan and Iran. Iranian Press TV reported: "Commander of the Aerospace Division of the Islamic Revolution Guards Corps (IRGC) Brigadier General Amir-Ali Hajizadeh said in December that all the data on the downed drone were 'fully decoded'."[3]

While the Pentagon evidently addressed the lack of encrypting feeds on ISR platforms after discovering the ease with which their downlinks could be captured, if Iran were able to "de-code" data found on board the RQ-170 this would demonstrate that either the encryption keys were obtainable from the onboard systems or the encryption for stored data was weak. Lack of end-to-end security in communications is a troubling indicator that the US procurement doctrine for weapons systems has not given much weight to cybersecurity.

Spoofing a GPS signal is relatively simple since locally generated signals can be much more powerful than signals transmitted from a satellite constellation. Todd Humphreys and a team from the University of Texas demonstrated how they could deflect a commercial drone off course with $3,000 worth of equipment and later made headlines when they demonstrated the same techniques on a 210-ft motor yacht.[4]

Iran's FAR news agency claimed Iran had downed another drone in February, 2013 with CNN reporting they claimed "IRGC's electronic warfare systems detected electronic signals, which indicated that foreign drones intended to enter our country", said Islamic Revolutionary Guards Corps Lt. Gen. Hamid Sarkheili. "Our specialist forces then succeeded in bringing down the drone in the field of maneuvers." Apparently two years after the original incident with the RQ-170, drone technology was still susceptible to jamming and redirecting through GPS spoofing.[5]

As drone warfare proliferates, attacks against their command and control as well as their navigation and intelligence streams will grow too. The number of countries with active drone development programs for ISR have grown to 76 in the past few years. In addition to the US, "Israel,... the United Kingdom, China and Iran appear to be the only other countries with operationally deployed armed drones."[6] The US will most likely be on the forefront of developing those attacks, but must look to ensuring that its own drone forces are protected.

In another incident, GPS jamming is credited with forcing a US Army RC-7B ARL (Airborne Reconnaissance Low) to make an emergency landing during the September 2011 Key Resolve-Foal Eagle exercise conducted in Korea. Drones are not the only platforms that have proven vulnerable to GPS jamming.[7]

STDMA issues and IFF

More evidence is available that network-centric military systems are being deployed without proper consideration of attack methodologies. Space-Time Division Multiple Access (STDMA) is a method of assigning frequencies and shuffling them in much the way that CDMA does for cell phones only with a geo-location element that assists when communication links traverse cells.[8] STDMA is the system used in commercial automatic identification systems (AIS) and widely deployed in civil marine applications.

Most ships are now tracked globally using this system, which bears a marked resemblance to military Identity Friend or Foe (IFF) transponder systems. Like many poorly designed authentication systems (SWIFT wire transfers, for instance) AIS relies on client side authentication. Client-side authentication means that the network trusts the client credentials that are presented. These systems are vulnerable to spoofing. The maritime AIS was abused by the Ramtin, an Iranian crude oil tanker, which masqueraded as another smaller ship registered out of the United Arab Emirates. This allowed it to avoid identification as it attempted to side-step sanctions imposed on Iran.[9]

Over 400,000 ships are tracked using the AIS system. Researchers at Trend Micro, a security vendor, demonstrated that "AIS is comprehensively vulnerable to a wide range of attacks that could be easily carried out by pirates, terrorists or other attackers."[10]

As early as 1997 the US Air Force was developing a system similar to AIS and using the same faulty protocols: FASSTAR.[11] Research is ongoing on integrating drones into the AIS system, even the Global Hawk high altitude drone has been fitted with commercial AIS,[12] one more instance of technologies that were developed with a lack of security foresight being integrated into modern weapons systems.

CHAPTER TWELVE

Systems Thinking

Systems thinking in security

Software Assurance is only one small component of devising systems that are not vulnerable to attack. End-to-end security takes a systems-level approach to design. While individual components may be secured using software assurance tools and methodologies, there are still potential vulnerabilities in the way each sub-system communicates with the others. A common error in so-called secure file storage systems is for the data to be encrypted in transit from an endpoint to a server via SSL. The web transport between a browser and a server is one component. But the web server decrypts the SSL traffic before re-encrypting the data for storage. That decryption phase could expose the clear text to capture. On top of that, many secure file systems encrypt every user's data with the same encryption key. If that key is compromised, every user's data is subject to being stolen or seized by law enforcement.

Secure communication between a drone operating over contested territory and its base is the simplest case to address. Video data is encrypted as it is captured and relayed through satellite, ground station, or airborne system to the flight operators who, in real time, are directing the drone and operating its sensors and fire control. As we have seen, even that level of protection was not built into most drone systems until after they were demonstrated to be vulnerable in 2009. Modern encryption protocols have additional benefits beyond protecting the confidentiality of communications. Availability and integrity are two qualities that are important to a defender. Integrity, in terms of data security, means that an attacker cannot inject unwanted data into the encrypted stream to, for instance, provide false information to or from a sensor.

Owens' vision for completely networked battle spaces is much more complicated than the simple case of a drone communicating with its ground-based command center. It would involve secure communications links between multiple interoperable systems.

Every link down the chain of command from the Advanced Extremely High Frequency (AEHF) geo-synchronous satellite constellation,[1] meant to allow the President to communicate anywhere in the world, to the Pentagon, to the battle group, to the commander in the field, to each of the individual combatants, has to be authenticated and encrypted. Every sensor on every platform (satellite, airborne, sea or ground-based) has to communicate securely, over several hops, with every platform that needs intelligence to create situational awareness. Fire control commands, to deliver precision munitions to their targets, have to be authenticated and of course encrypted. Once the secure channel is in place it has to be "re-keyed" periodically and in an emergency when a key is compromised.

Satellite operators are beginning to think in terms of end-to-end security. The chief information security officer of Intelsat, speaking at a 2014 conference said: "...hybrid systems increase the avenues intruders can use to steal data, overwhelm a system to deny service, or otherwise infer with communications. ...When you combine satellite and terrestrial, you are actually magnifying the threat vectors exponentially."[2]

This level of communication security, especially the ability to manage the distribution of keys is in its infancy. There is no evidence that the relatively young KMIP (Key Management Interoperability Protocol) standards that would be required have been widely adopted in military systems.[3] Rather, manual updates for rekeying are the norm. The loss of a single system, a drone, a communication device, or a computer (as in the 2001 EP-3E incident) causes an expensive and time-consuming effort to update and replace platforms.

Security Systems thinking has yet to percolate through the military procurement process—and is unlikely to until there is a disastrous military failure due to cyber attack.

CHAPTER THIRTEEN

Electronic Warfare

Electronic Warfare and cyber

If there is one component of the NCW fighting force that has seen considerable investment over decades, it is Electronic Warfare (EW). Continuous improvement in RF jamming ability and counter EW have been the norm. A recent review in the *Los Angeles Times* claims the Chinese PLA is known to have "poured money into electronic warfare and has publicly acknowledged conducting training exercises. Such exercises are such a concern for the Air Force that it has been training fighter and bomber pilots to fly without GPS, data links, communications and radar." In other words, pilots are being trained to fight without the benefits of NCW capabilities. The article goes on to quote General Mike Hostage, commander of Air Combat Command, in September, 2013:

> "Our adversaries have taken careful note and have been investing in asymmetric ways to deny us these systems. Our adversaries should know that such asymmetric attacks will not stop us; they will only make us mad."[1]

Indeed, one may ask, why wait to get mad? The early warning signs are there and a forward thinking approach would be to build defenses in now.

Cyberwar and EW have been conjoined only once according to

sparse reports. While cyberwar deals exclusively with the digital domain, it is apparently possible using RF to inject code into the fire control systems of Russian ground-to-air missile batteries. Writing in *Aviation Week & Space Technology*, David A. Fulghum reported that Israel used such a capability to shut down Syria's missile defense system during the incursion to destroy Syria's Al Kibar nuclear reactor on September 6, 2007.[2] Referring to BAE Systems' SUTER airborne network attack program:

"The technology allows users to invade communications networks, see what enemy sensors see and even take over as systems administrator so sensors can be manipulated into positions so that approaching aircraft can't be seen, they say. The process involves locating enemy emitters with great precision and then directing data streams into them that can include false targets and misleading messages algorithms that allow a number of activities including control."[3]

This capability may have been confirmed when reports arose that President Obama considered a similar operation against Libyan radar systems during the NATO strikes against Libya, while the *Los Angeles Times* points out, "The U.S. Navy used EA-18 Growler jets in 2011 to jam Libyan dictator Moammar Kadafi's ground radar, enabling NATO fighters and bombers to strike tanks, communication depots and other targets with complete freedom."[4]

The New York Times reported in October of 2011 that the US had contemplated cyberwar against Libya:

"While the exact techniques under consideration remain classified, the goal would have been to break through the firewalls of the Libyan government's computer networks to sever military communication links and prevent the early-warning radars from gathering information and relaying it to missile batteries aiming at NATO warplanes." The White House decided not to set a precedent of using such cyber means to disable Libyan air defenses and opted to use conventional jamming and targeting of radar sites.[5]

Fulghum reported that the boundary between EW and cyber warfare has been eroded. Quoting a "veteran electronic attack specialist" he wrote:

"'I'm putting a cyber-signal into the emission that makes the target [sensor] think the signal is something else – perhaps a group of approaching aircraft,' the specialist says. 'Cyber is what happens when the spoofing signal gets to the receiver of the target network. That receiver may see false signals or it may provide an access port that you can get information out of [with malware]."[6]

Conversations with people familiar with such techniques reveal that the enemy radar is treated as a black box. In a laboratory setting a series of signals are sent that cover a broad spectrum of possible formats, a process very similar to network "fuzzing" attacks. The resultant signals generated by the radar receiver are examined. At the simplest level, if a 1 or 0 can be created then any stream of data can be produced. From there, a vulnerability in the receiver could be used to execute code and infect the system and the adjoining network.

As with any attack vector the concept of injecting code through a port highlights the need for addition protections. Firewalls, Intrusion Prevention Systems, and malware defences, in radar systems are needed.

CHAPTER FOURTEEN

Gathering Cyber Storm

From RMA to CRMA

While the debate over the Revolution in Military Affairs, which reached its peak just before 9/11, has not been resolved, technology has been introduced into the battle space that accomplishes at least some of the goals promulgated by the adherents to RMA. Cebrowski, Owens, and others have their claims on the vision of a networked fighting force that would:

1. Reduce the fog of war through complete situational awareness derived from a sensor grid consisting of ground, air, sea, and space based ISR platforms.
2. Allow the dissemination of command and control from the top down while giving the war fighter the ability to work autonomously.
3. Benefit from the force multiplier of precision-guided weapons that could find their targets with pinpoint accuracy, reducing collateral damage, and ensuring rapid achievement of goals.

Yet the vision for network-centric war fighting has been executed with a blind eye to the inherent vulnerabilities that come from interoperability and relying on computer systems and communication technology (that have almost infinite attack surface, as measured by flaws in software) and trust relationships that are indefensible.

The Department of Defense Strategy for Cyberspace is telling.

The July 2011 document defines the problem its strategy addresses as:

"DoD operates over 15,000 networks and seven million computing devices across hundreds of installations in dozens of countries around the globe. DoD uses cyberspace to enable its military, intelligence, and business operations, including the movement of personnel and material and the command and control of the full spectrum of military operations."[1] In other words the strategy and the DoD's cyberspace operations are no more than the network IT security function of a very large organization.

The Quadrennial Defense Review 2014 is remarkably silent on the need for software assurance practices in the defense acquisition process. Cyber defense is still viewed in terms of cyberspace and network defense and attacks:

"The Department of Defense will deter, and when approved by the President and directed by the Secretary of Defense, will disrupt and deny adversary cyberspace operations that threaten U.S. interests. To do so, we must be able to defend the integrity of our own networks, protect our key systems and networks, conduct effective cyber operations overseas when directed, and defend the Nation from an imminent, destructive cyberattack on vital U.S. interests."[2]

According to a March 5, 2014 Air Force Instruction, one such approval from the President and Secretary of Defense for conducting military cyberspace operations was issued on June 21, 2013.[3] The revelation of the Execute Order (EXORD) is the first indication that the US is engaging in cyber military operations of an offensive nature, although the target and goals of the operation are yet to be discovered.[4]

The 2015 National Security Strategy, the second of Obama's

administration, is replete with mentions of cyber security, but all mentions are of the risk to business and critical infrastructure. This document, which is already being termed the "Strategic Patience" doctrine thanks to its attempt at creating a narrative of the Obama Presidency's foreign relations legacy, will be looked back on as oblivious to the threats against the US's ability to project force thanks to its military's vulnerability to cyber effects.

The newly appointed Director of the Defense Intelligence Agency (DIA) Lieutenant General, U.S. Marine Corps Vincent R. Stewart, had this to say when he presented his first Worldwide Threat Assessment to Congress, in February, 2015:

"The global cyber threat environment presents numerous persistent challenges to the security and integrity of DoD networks and information. Threat actors now demonstrate an increased ability and willingness to conduct aggressive cyberspace operations—including both service disruptions and espionage—against U.S. and allied defense information networks."[5]

Stewart was elevated to the DIA from his position as head of the US Marine Force Cyber Command. Nowhere in his threat assessment was there any acknowledgement that there were threats against US war fighting ability due to vulnerabilities in systems. That will come with time.

Weapons and communications systems that were designed before there was acknowledgement of these vulnerabilities are at risk of being impacted by cyber attacks during future conflicts. The US military, despite its demonstrated dominance in the field of computer network exploitation and attack (as revealed by the NSA's catalog of tools), has been slow to adjust to a new reality because of a lack of exposure to battlefield attacks against these vulnerabilities. The capture of drones by Iran and North Korea and the interception of unencrypted traffic from drones in Iraq and Afghanistan could have served as a wake up call, but based on lack of discussion of widespread weaknesses in the literature, it is evident that it will require much more to change the specification and acquisition process to a point where software assurance is embedded in the end-to-end supply chain.

Just as Cebrowksi lauded the use of email and video conferencing by Admiral Clemins during the Taiwan Straits incident, it is possible to predict a similar future scenario when an adversary disrupts or confuses digital communication and GPS location data, denies command and control, disables aircraft and ships, and destroys the ability of a fighting force.

In 2012 Secretary of Defense Leon Panetta warned of a "digital Pearl Harbor." He meant to evoke an image of devastating attacks on the US power grid and other critical infrastructure.[6] But the proper scenario, one that evokes a military failure on the scale of that at Pearl Harbor, would be a military engagement where an adversary completely disabled the fighting forces of the United States to achieve victory. In my opening chapter I chose to use a replay of the 1995-6 Taiwan Straits Crisis to illustrate the possible repercussions. An engagement in Eastern Europe between Russia and NATO forces, or a skirmish between North and South Korea, or an incursion into Iraq by Iran, could be equally revealing.

While the debate over a late 1990s RMA may not have been resolved, a future conflict between technologically advanced powers where one effectively uses cyber attacks to deny, disrupt, disable, or destroy the other's war fighting ability will be hailed as the CRMA: the Cyber Revolution in Military Affairs.

CHAPTER FIFTEEN

Looking Back, Looking Forward

The history of "cybersecurity as an afterthought" cannot be denied. Drawing from that history it is a foregone conclusion that modern precision weapons systems, the foundation of future US war fighting ability in advanced ships, drones, jet fighters, bombers, radar, satellite comms, and sensors will all be fraught with vulnerabilities. These vulnerabilities will be targeted by adversaries when the time is right. The ability of the US military to project force is in jeopardy.

There is always a reluctance on the part of a modern attacker to use an exploit for tactical advantage. Once used, a cyber weapon quickly becomes ineffective for future use as the victim discovers the targeted vulnerability and deploys corrections.

Sadly, most military organizations' procurement processes are so cumbersome that corrections take time and are horrendously expensive. The types of brute force responses seen to date are clear indicators of what the future holds. The reaction to the Agent.btz worm that spread through SIPRNet was corrected by the sledgehammer approach of re-imaging every computer that could have been impacted. Reported cost: $1 billion. The loss of the NSA's secure OS in a downed spy plane exposed supposedly secure comms for seven years. When the Chinese tipped their hand that they could decrypt military traffic on the occasion of Obama winning the 2008 election, it cost over $100 million to re-key and deploy new software in the field. A reported incursion into the email servers of the Pentagon also cost $100 million to clean up.

Reactive measures are always more costly than building it right the first time. Money saved on building shoddy freeways or bridges always pushes the real costs into the future at much greater pain and possible loss of life.

But active measures can be effective if they are thought out beforehand and applied as soon as a new vulnerability, a new risk, appears on the horizon. One likes to think that the discovery of a new Near Earth Orbiting object—an asteroid—on a collision course with the Earth, would lead to a massive effort to find a solution. With enough time the application of a small continuous force, such as the ion engines used for interplanetary travel today, could change the future trajectory of the asteroid. The shorter the time before impact the greater the force that must be applied.

The US military has already had its early warning, many of them in fact. Drones led astray due to unauthenticated GPS signals. Ships using spoofed AIS identities. Streaming video from drones decrypted by insurgents. Worms spreading through SIPRNet.

One potentially positive event in the near future would be if an adversary tipped his hand. Russian forces in Ukraine could use cyber effects to blind a fighter jet in combat. North Korea could demonstrate widespread cyber vulnerability in US technology during the annual joint Foal Eagle exercise with South Korea and the US. The hope would be that whatever the event it would spark a rapid response, the type spelled out in this chapter.

Even the possibility of the enemy tipping their hand early does not change the fact that it is not hard to predict, as this book does, that in the near future there will be a devastating use of cyber attack against military systems; a true cyber Pearl Harbor. An event that will have dramatic and expensive impacts.

Heads will roll. There will be Congressional inquiries. Generals and admirals will be paraded in front of hearings. New laws will be passed with little dissent and even less thought. Development of weapons systems will be delayed by years. The likely first step is a mandate that all military and government procurement procedures will be modified to include terms that refer to software assurance. A new hierarchy of consultants and contractors will arise to help the Defense Industrial Base meet these requirements.

Ultimately the cost to harden all ISR, comms, and weapons systems could exceed a trillion dollars and programs will be delayed.

The alternative would be to look ahead and effect the required changes starting today. To comprehend what that would involve, here are several steps that if enacted now, could avoid future cyber military disasters.

Encryption and Key Management

The military makes wide use of encryption just as corporations and individuals do. And just as the general use of encryption is fraught with complications for all parties, the military has demonstrated that it does not have a comprehensive ability to encrypt everything and manage keys. Massive leaks of top secret material to trusted insiders like Private Bradley Manning and Edward Snowden are just one indicator that the DoD and even the NSA still rely on a system of compartmentalization and trust to protect documents.

Trust reinforced by background checks (when they are done well, as opposed to the shortcuts taken by USIS, the outside contractor that was responsible for Snowden's background check and has since been found negligent in thousands of cases), periodic polygraph tests, and monitoring of personnel activity on the network, has proved itself effective. The occurrence of only two major leaks (that we know about) indicate that considering the million-plus people with top security clearances, the intelligence community and the military have systems in place that discourage widespread leaks. Of course out of that million-plus the chances of more than one being a foreign agent is pretty good considering the history of infiltration over the years. And we only know of those who have been caught.

The intelligence and diplomatic corps aside, there is an immediate need to design and deploy a comprehensive, resilient, and dependable encryption scheme across all battle commands.

Most forward operating bases have a cumbersome means of managing keys. During the Iraq War a simple satellite phone or communications handset would be issued to a combatant with encryption keys authorized and installed. When that soldier was rotated out of Iraq after a six-month deployment, his or her replacement would have to request a key, the NSA would approve and create the key, and pass it down the chain of command to the nearest CommSec office. The guy who needs it drives to CommSec, picks up keys, drives back and loads keys (up to 50 depending on the number of networks) in communication devices, weapons platforms, and ISR gear. Because keys are rarely revoked or removed by the operator, over time that equipment could end up with as many as 200 keys on it. If lost or captured that device could communicate over all the networks it had ever been assigned to!

While the Commands should share methods, the actual encryption, key management, and infrastructure, should be compartmentalized. The problem that Owen discovered during his command has yet to be addressed. There is no apparent method for communicating between services, let alone with allied partners and their services. A comprehensive standard for authentication and encryption of communication links should be as simple to use as a phone system or Skype is today.

After the Chinese capture of the keys from the NSA's secure computers on the Navy spy plane, the NSA has embarked on a program to improve key management, called KMS, to replace the cumbersome manual method of EKMI. Of course the NSA is more concerned with CommSec than the encryption required for munitions and ISR platforms. Deploying key management to the myriad weapons platforms is most likely to be done on a "going forward" basis. Revamping key management for existing platforms would be very expensive as new software, and sometimes hardware, would need to be sourced, developed, and deployed to the field.

Communications channels between sensors, authentication of Command and Control signals, and positive identification of drones, weapons, and platforms should be standard and universal in deployment.

Device authentication technology that is commonly available in the commercial arena could be incorporated into military hardware. A Trusted Platform Module, a hardened chip on every device that stores a chain of trust from manufacturer to owner, should be built into every device that has a computer that communicates via any network.

The practice, evident in the revelations of vulnerable drones, of storing encryption keys on drones, cruise missiles, and even satellite phones, has to stop.

Supply Chain Hardening

The purpose of cyber supply chain assurance is to use procedures at every step of the manufacture and delivery of software and hardware that prevents the introduction of malware, flaws, vulnerabilities, and backdoors in components of weapons platforms, C&C communication gear, ISR, and munitions.

The core of the new encryption regime has to be trustworthy hardware in the form of "roots of trust," or microchips. An attacker could poison that root of trust if they could get at the manufacture of those chips or somehow intercept them and swap them out for modified counterfeit chips (*interdiction*). The same goes for any hardware components.

There is a myth, never verified, of the Manchurian Chip. One variant of the story is that a contractor called in to review the computer systems on board the M1A1 Abrams Tank was surprised to find a whole section of the motherboard that did not appear on any design schematics. On further investigation it appeared that the new circuitry would allow an attacker to use WiFi to control the fuel injectors to the tank engine, specifically to force it to a crawl in a battle theater. While the matter may be relegated to the same collection of stories that include the one told by Gus W. Weiss and repeated by William Safire about the Farewell Dossier and the US slipping faulty components into a Soviet pipeline causing an explosion picked up by reconnaissance satellites, the Manchurian Chip is useful as a metaphor for the entire realm of supply chain attacks.

Addressing the Manchurian Chip issue means drastic changes to supply chain management. At the board level it may mean 100%

inspection of motherboards and auxiliary boards visually. Luckily the manufacturers themselves have led the development of machine vision inspection as a quality control measure. Deploying automated visual systems to check for the existence of new or changed components is expensive, but a service provider or large integrator could provide that and take additional measures post-inspection to ensure that the computer or network gear arrived in an untampered state. Many of the ANT catalog bugs are physical components added to networking gear from Cisco, Juniper, and Wauwei. Visual inspection would catch these.

A new vendor of hardened servers, Skyport Systems, takes a photo of the inside of their appliances before shipping, encrypts and digitally signs the image, and embeds it on the TPM. This is the first anti-interdiction system introduced post-Snowden.

There are at least three ways to inspect silicon chips such as CPUs and signal processors for unwarranted modifications. The first is destructive, so rather difficult to integrate into a supply chain solution. The chips are chemically etched and x-rayed to expose their circuitry. The resulting diagram is compared to the original design. No changes, no worries. Of course, a determined hacker could infiltrate the design process and insert his desired changes early in the development cycle. The second method of chip verification is a timing test. It is based on the assumption that the time to perform a series of common functions of the chip would change if the chip design had been tampered with. This too can be destructive because the chip inputs and outputs have to be accessed directly.

A third way was recently developed by PFP Cybersecurity of Vienna, VA. Their solution is based on the behavior of the chip during normal operation. They have a small device that is set in close proximity to the chip and reads electromagnetic emissions that they then correlate with power consumption. It is based on the theory that the signature will change if the chip acts abnormally; as it would if it contained a backdoor or some other malicious change.[1]

System Hardening

Most of the reported breaches of military systems by outsiders can be diagnosed as poor endpoint protection. Since cyber espionage is a rapidly evolving battleground unto itself, every measure must be taken to increase the time, difficulty, and cost to the attacker. The computers and network gear used by the military must be hardened to the maximum technical feasibility. This starts with a hardened operating system.

Most of the DoD computers used for office work are still WindowsXP, an OS with a history of vulnerabilities which is no longer supported by Microsoft, although some customers continue to pay for support. While the DoD contemplates upgrading it should give thought to getting off of Windows altogether. While Windows 10, the latest version, is considered to be fairly robust, the issue is that DoD systems should not participate in the same ecosystem of vulnerabilities as the rest of the world.

Just as a forest comprised of all the same species of trees is subject to mass extinction by the invasion of a single pest, a computing ecosystem comprised of machines that experience the same vulnerabilities is always at risk. Most of the endpoint-protection industry is dedicated to protecting Windows computers. Hackers, hacktivists, cybercriminals, and nation-states take advantage of this homogeneity by reusing exploits that work in one arena against another.

If the DoD had a completely different OS as the basis of their desktop computing and servers they would not have to expend all the resources they do today fighting infections and continuously patching. If and when an attack occurred they would know immediately that it was a targeted attack meant for DoD systems. Take that to the next step and deploy different operating systems for different purposes and even for different branches and, at the very least, the attackers would be forced to expend more time and money developing tailored attacks. There are plenty of platforms available today that could supplant the dominant Windows: Apple OS X for desktops and laptops. Linux for servers. FreeBSD or another flavor of Unix for special servers, Chrome for tablets, and IOS for smart phones.

The admittedly large sums that would be needed to revamp computing in the military would be dominated by transitioning critical applications to the new platform. This cost is the primary reason that the DoD has not moved away from XP. It is a problem shared by banks, manufacturers, and critical infrastructure providers.

One aspect of ubiquitous networking that the DoD has moved to relentlessly is that applications can move to cloud services. In this way, the DoD and those contractors that support their computing environment can invest in transitioning these services and earn the advantages of the cloud that most commercial application providers are doing. Instead of having to maintain code and issue new releases, causing a software update requirement with its accompanying vulnerability management issues, a cloud application can be fixed once and every user gets the new features, bug fixes, and protection from a repaired vulnerability.

A common cloud architecture with standard server images is also easier to maintain and fix. If a particular server suffers a glitch, it is erased and a new server is created on the fly. The attacker cannot as easily maintain a persistent presence.

Separating applications from endpoints means that it is easier to have a heterogeneous device environment. An Apple MacBook running Safari can access Gmail as easily as a smart phone, tablet, or new platform.

While weapons systems and handheld communication devices typically do not run Windows, there has not been enough effort put into hardening them. They have taken advantage of being outside the Windows ecosystem so have not suffered from common malware. This has served the military well. But this is security by obscurity. It relies on the absence of a motivated attacker. In the new reality of future cyberwar this will no longer be the case.

Operational Hardening

While beefing up defenses in the combatant commands is critical to successful use of armed forces, the astoundingly poor state of security practices within the Pentagon and business operations of the military have to be addressed. The DoD and other government agencies that work with or direct the DoD must play significant catch-up just to keep pace with advanced capabilities of many private organizations.

Continuous Network Monitoring

The DoD has entered on a decade long program to reduce the number of connections to the Internet. The original Trusted Internet Connection (TIC) goal, as stated in M-08-05 – Implementation of Trusted Internet Connection, was to reduce

15,000 connections to 50. By May, 2008 there were still 2,758 Internet connections.[2] The next step, dubbed Einstein I, was to deploy IDS at each of these gateways. IDS is merely a passive alerting system that matches network traffic to a signature database (the most popular maintained by the open source SNORT community) and generating a log entry when a match is found. The IDS devices connect to a tap on the network without taking any action to block or deny malicious traffic. An enhancement to IDS is IPS (Intrusion Prevention), which is what Einstein II is supposed to use.

Constant successful attacks even against networks with IDS and IPS have demonstrated that more is needed. Technology that can provide continuous network monitoring has to be deployed everywhere, not just at the gateway, but throughout the network so that all traffic can be monitored.

There are two primary technologies for Continuous Network Monitoring: flow monitoring and full network packet capture and analysis. Flow monitoring is easier to deploy and maintain. Most network routers and switches can report on network flow. Netflow and Sflow are two protocols that simply report every network connection and measure volumes of traffic. Monitoring tools gather all the flow data and alert on unusual behavior such as that seen when an infected host communicates with a command and control server or the lateral movement typical of an attacker's activity once they have established a foothold.

Full packet capture and analysis is even more powerful, but entails a large investment in storage. A feed of threat intelligence data can be run against the captured network traffic to determine if there are signs of an attack underway.

Both methods of continuous network monitoring would have caught the spread of Agent.btz across SIPRNet as soon as it was introduced at a forward operating base in the Mideast.

Continuous network monitoring can also determine when a trusted insider engages in unusual behavior, such as that of Edward Snowden when he was collecting NSA files from his office in Hawaii.

Cyber Force Transformation Czar

Cebrowski's Office of Force Transformation still resides within the Pentagon. One could argue that it succeeded in some part of its mission to put the US military on a NCW footing. Now it is time to appoint a Cyber Force Transformation Czar to fill Cebrowski's position and institute the necessary cyber protections to enable network war fighting to be effective.

The Cyber Force Transformation Czar would be responsible for orchestrating the changes itemized here. The person picked to fill the role should come from industry in much the same way Robert McNamara and his "bright boys" were plucked from Ford Motor Company to transition the military to a Cold War footing against a single adversary. This person and his or her mission would have to have complete support from the Executive branch and the Secretary of Defense.

The most effective means of wielding power for change in the Pentagon is by holding the purse strings. The Cyber Czar would have to be empowered to hold up funding for weapons platforms until they could be certified as being impervious to cyber attack. NIST, if given the chance would be the ideal body to create those requirements, while the Czar would enforce them.

CHAPTER SIXTEEN

The Dangers of Risk Management

One of the most damaging ideas in cyber defense is that of risk management principles applied to IT security. Since Donald Rumsfeld came back to government for his second stint as Secretary of Defense, the DoD and the primary body for setting security standards, NIST, have been permeated with risk management thinking. Most cybersecurity legislation, as proposed, and many Presidential Directives as well, call for "Risk Management Principles" to be adopted. NIST's Cybersecurity Framework is heavily slanted towards risk management.

While few small businesses have formal risk management programs, most large business do. They even have risk committees that are drawn from the board of directors, often headed by the CFO. The goal is to identify risks to the business and either reduce their potential impact with compensating controls, or purchase insurance to offset the business risk.

For example, a large airline, thanks to its risk management program, may recognize rising fuel prices could hurt its competitiveness and decide to hedge fuel on the open market, or a car manufacturer that has gone too far down the path of Just-In-Time supply may start to warehouse critical components in case a supplier in Thailand is wiped out by a flood.

But try to translate risk management theories to IT and you run into troubles. Every risk management program starts with the dictate to identify all IT assets and weight them based on their criticality to business operations. The next step is to reduce "surface area of attack" by discovering vulnerabilities in those systems and patching or protecting them. Let's look at why these steps are doomed to failure:

1. It is expensive and nearly impossible to identify all IT assets.

While at first glance identifying assets appears to be a simple problem, it is actually extremely complex, almost fractally complex. IT assets include every computer (desktop, laptop, server, print server), every application (database, email, ERP), every data set (customer lists, earth resources data, product pricing guide), all email, all documents in all versions, all identities and all communications.

Now, add in the proliferation of devices coming in with consumerization — smartphones, iPads, even e-readers — and the data that reside on them. Then add in the dynamic nature of the cloud, where servers can be in a constant state of flux as load is elastically met with more or fewer virtual machines. As the military continues down its path to network everything, a path promulgated by Arthur Cebrowski, everything becomes part of the IT risk management paradigm.

The next big problem?

2. It is impossible to assign value to IT assets.

The concept behind IT risk management is that you assign a value to each asset. There are many algorithms for doing so. It usually involves a cross-functional team meeting and making at least high-level determinations. But it is obviously impossible to assign a dollar value to each IT asset. Is it the cost of replacing the asset? That might work for a lumberyard, but an email server might have a replacement value of $2,000 while the potential damage to a company from losing access to email for an extended period could be millions of dollars in terms of lost productivity, let alone the costs associated with the content of emails being stolen and leaked.

What about the value of each email? How much is one email worth? Ten cents? Zero? What about the internal email between the Joint Chiefs and the Combatant Commands as they get ready to launch an operation? Its dollar value is zero, but the risk from that email getting into the wrong hands could be the loss of tactical or strategic advantage.

Most organizations give up on the dollar value asset ranking and come up with low-medium-high valuations. The task is at least as difficult as a sequestration summit to decide which programs and which departments get cut.

3. Risk management methods invariably fail to predict the actual disasters.

While many risk management programs focus on personally identifiable information like credit cards or health records for various regulatory regimes, the problem of protecting the types of information that reside in government or military enclaves is much harder. Of course the continuous breaches of credit card data indicate just how successful risk management has been at protecting those simple to define data sets. If risk management were a successful way to avoid breaches there would be much fewer of them reported. Weapons designs, source code, military movements and logistics do not fall into any regulatory regime.

An example of another hole in risk management systems is their failure to update to reflect present-day: A giant financial services data center located on the Gulf Coast of Florida used risk management techniques. Among the usual list — power failure, Internet outage, fire — was a line item for a hurricane with a storm surge of greater than 20 feet (the level above sea level of the berm surrounding the data center). Because there had not been a single such storm in 100 years this received a risk rating of 9 out of 10, with 10 being the least likely. An FDIC auditor pointed out that in that particular year there had been four such storm surges to hit the Gulf Coast. The data center risk profile had never been revisited to reflect a changing environment.

Nasim Talib has ruffled feathers in the financial markets by developing his theory of Black Swan events–those that no risk management regime can predict and that have usually disastrous results. The dramatic stock market crash of 1987 is one such example. The Global Financial Crisis of 2008 is another. IT risk management programs suffer from the same inability to predict outliers. Society General, one of the largest financial institutions in the world, had controls in place to reduce the risk of a single trader exposing it to large trading losses. They did not account for a Gerome Kervial who bypassed those controls to hide his $50 billion exposure in commodities. When it was discovered and his positions sold off for a loss of $7 billion SocGen had to announce those losses in January of 2009, doing nothing to calm already roiled markets worldwide.

JP Morgan Chase, a bank with a well established risk management program, both for financial exposure and for IT risks, failed to foresee or "manage" the risk associated with the most sophisticated attackers who managed to steal a digital certificate for an internal event website that was used to further penetrate their operations. The result was the loss of 76 million household customer identities. This from an organization that claims to spend $250 million annually on IT security. JP Morgan was not even aware of the breach until they were presented with data from a small consultant in Chicago.

The disastrous attack on Sony Entertainment is perhaps one of the clearest examples of how risk management fails. Sony had certainly learned from experience as it was a frequent target of attack. In 2005 Sony included spyware in a software distribution for one of its games. After Sony sued George Hotz, a proficient hacker, for breaking protections of the Play Station game console, the Sony Play Station Network was subjected to massive Denial of Service attacks from hackers loosely associated with Anonymous, the catch-all collective of digital protesters. Under cover of the DDoS attack, when presumably Sony security and network administrators were focused elsewhere, a splinter group called Lulzsec infiltrated Sony and stole 24.6 million user IDs, passwords, and credit card details. In the wake of that attack Sony hired Phil Rietinger away from his position at the National Cyber Security Center (NCSC) and appointed him CISO. Now with a CISO to establish a risk management program the risk from DDoS could be addressed. The risk of a data breach could be addressed. But what about the risk of a nation-state, the DPRK, taking umbrage to the planned release of Seth Brogan's *The Interview*?

The FBI, NSA, and President Obama have all gone on record attributing the Sony breach to North Korea. While several vendor research teams have pointed fingers at insiders, or Russia, or both, being involved in the breach, they fail to realize that the NSA, in addition to building a massive surveillance machine, have also created a massive attribution engine. With access to most data traversing the Internet the NSA has better data than even a large security vendor can gather from its sensors.

The breach of Sony in November, 2014 was the most dramatic

and debilitating up to that time. Even months later there is evidence that the cleanup has not been completed. The attackers, communicating with executives, threatened dire consequences unless *The Interview*, a silly comedy based on a plot to assassinate Kim Jong-un, was withheld from theaters. Sony capitulated, claiming that the theater chains had asked them not to release the film. Sony then recanted after the President expressed his disappointment with Sony for bowing to extortion demands. Meanwhile the attackers released four stolen movies, and embarrassing emails between executives. On March 31, 2015 the CEO of Sony Entertainment stepped down.

We have the benefit of those leaked emails, which included the results of a security audit performed by PricewaterhouseCoopers, to see what kind of security controls Sony had in place. After the PlayStation Network attacks Sony had embarked on a project to take over the monitoring of critical assets such as firewalls and servers that they had previously outsourced. That monitoring, primarily of logs and alerts, is symptomatic of risk management regimes where logging is to this day considered an effective security measure. The PwC audit reported that even the task of on-boarding log management had not been completed at the time of the breach.

It is the changing nature of threats that is impacting risk regimes today. IT assets that were not of interest to an experimental hacker in 1999 can be of extreme interest to a cybercriminal operation in Eastern Europe or a nation-state looking to leapfrog a Western competitor. It is impossible to know beforehand which IT assets will be of interest to an attacker, without knowing the adversary's interests.

4. Risk management devolves to "protect everything."

For risk management to work it has to be comprehensive, so comprehensive protections are deployed. Firewalls, IPS, and AV everywhere and vulnerability management (VM) systems deployed to check the exposure of every single device on the network. Vulnerability management has to be continuous because new vulnerabilities are announced every month for just about every application, OS and device.

A patch management system is then used to ensure that every application has the latest patch. Risk management methodologies strive for that golden state when no vulnerabilities exist anywhere. And, failing that, the desire is to minimize the total exposure time to new vulnerabilities. Organizations spend an inordinate amount of time and money on these protections. Of course, they still succumb to targeted attacks that use previously unknown (zero day) vulnerabilities.

So, what should organizations do? Use threat management techniques, not risk management.

CHAPTER SEVENTEEN

Threat Management

Consider if the US president's morning intelligence briefing was focused on risk management.

It would have to take into account the 40 or so US facilities that are involved in the production of nuclear weapons. Then there may be the 250 or so diplomatic missions around the world, and of course hundreds of US military bases, and maybe a breakdown of the 17 designated critical infrastructure sectors, not forgetting parks and national monuments and yes, movie studios.

Ridiculous, of course, because a true risk management report would summarize all of that information into a simple score. A vast army of risk auditors would be engaged to come up with a uniform scoring system and every "asset" would be given a score which would be weighted and rolled up into a dashboard that gave a single-pane-of-glass view into overall risk every day.

But if such a thing were even possible, what would it have shown the day before the USS *Cole* was attacked? Or on Sept. 10, 2001? Would it have acknowledged the risk of the rise of ISIS? Or Russia moving into Crimea? Global affairs are subject to Black Swans.

Of course a POTUS intelligence briefing is not about assets; it is about threat actors. Intelligence is gathered about their intentions, capabilities, and movements. Decisions are made based on *threats*. Real and present dangers are identified and resources are deployed to gather further intelligence (detect), deny, disrupt, delay, degrade, deceive or destroy the threat actors.

That is the basis of threat management, an approach that is proving to be much more effective at reducing the losses from targeted attacks. Enterprise IT security is moving that way with the creation of a new category of cyber defenses. At one level are startups that monitor threat actor activities globally. Companies like iSIGHT Partners infiltrate hacker and cybercriminal discussion forums and create play books of their methodologies and tools. Organizations apply those play books to their own environments. They monitor their networks for suspicious activity that matches the playbook. They subscribe to threat feeds that provide data on Indicators of Compromise (IoC) that can be matched with network traffic and endpoint infections. Threat feeds are generated by research companies that usually operate a global network of honey pots. Honey pots are computers and email accounts that are put on the Internet and are the recipients of numerous attacks. AV companies have long operated honey pot email accounts to supplement the intelligence they gather from their millions of users. Email attachments received by the honey pot accounts are opened, any embedded links are visited and attachments are allowed to execute. The intelligence from these attacks can include new malware samples, source IP addresses of spammers and destination IP addresses of C&C servers. That data is collated and streamed to subscribers who in turn monitor traffic and endpoints for any indication that they are under attack.

The ecosystem of that management has grown dramatically since the APT1 report from Mandiant set the industry in motion. That report, for the first time provided convincing detail that Chinese PLA operatives were engaging in full time cyber espionage. Detecting the attacks quickly and responding effectively has become the focus of most of the new security vendors.

The threat research community has created standards to help communicate the key Indicators of Compromise (IoC) they discover. STIX and TAXII are the protocols for communicating IP addresses, domains, and MD5 hashes (digital fingerprints) of malware and malicious files. There are open source and commercial subscriptions of such feeds that are quickly moving to STIX and TAXII.

Vendor such as ThreatStream and BrightPoint have even created threat intelligence management platforms that consumes multiple feeds, normalizes them, and then facilitates the integration with security tools such as SIEM to determine if any of the threat intelligence generates a "sighting," an alert that the enterprise is under attack. In the other direction, BrightPoint allows their customers to join "trust circles" within which they can share information and determine if a particular threat indicator has been sighted by other community members.

Security Analytics (SA) is becoming an important capability in threat management. SIEM data and network traffic is examined, parsed, and analyzed to recognize when an attack is under way. Early practitioners of SA had to use various labor-intensive tools to do these functions, but new companies like Prelert, Sqrrl, and Lightcyber, are automating the process.

While risk management demands that an organization track an infinite exposure, threat management can focus on several categories of actors:

Insiders take advantage of their authorized access to computers, networks, and applications for their own advantage. They may be the "disgruntled employee" who merely wishes to cause damage. Take for example Jason Cornish, who had set up mission-critical virtual machines for Shionogi, a subsidiary of a

Japanese pharmaceutical company that has offices in New Jersey and Georgia. When his friend was terminated Cornish quit the company, drove down the road to the nearest McDonald's and logged in over its free WiFi to erase those virtual servers. Thanks to a remarkably effective FBI, it did not take long to trace the activity to the AT&T WiFi access point at the McDonald's and confirm that the disgruntled insider had purchased a Big Mac with his credit card shortly before the destruction.

Addressing the insider threat has always been one of the primary purposes of computer and network security. Remember IBM's RACF? Yet, most organizations rely on written contracts and policies or implicit trust to prevent employee and contractor abuse.

Network monitoring and employee activity monitoring, which usually entails an agent deployed to desktops to record all actions, should be deployed to deter insider misbehavior. A robust Identity and Access Management (IAM) solution will also help. Strong authentication to establish identity and then the ability to revoke access when an employee leaves or a contractor is no longer needed should also be mandated.

Hackers get a lot of press. They tend to target vulnerable systems just to demonstrate their hacking prowess. Countering hackers is the realm of one aspect of traditional risk management. Frequent external scans for vulnerabilities and an active effort to patch those vulnerabilities is the best defense. Putting a firewall and other defenses in front of Internet-facing assets is another requirement. The principle of being uninteresting to a hacker by not having easily exploited vulnerabilities applies, much as one discourages neighborhood burglaries by installing motion sensing floodlights and good locks.

Cyber criminals are the primary concern of any organization that handles money. Banks, mortgage brokers, stock trading desks, and even the CFO or administrator responsible for wire transfers at a small enterprise, are all targets. Being familiar with trends and immediate activities of cyber criminals may be enough warning to bolster defenses. Just as TJX could have learned from the Lowe's attack via Pringles-enhanced WiFi, Target Corp could have seen the attack coming by monitoring the rise of PoS malware.

Nation-state attacks against corporations, universities, and government research labs can be traced back decades, but they began to be common in 2004 with the discovery of multiple breaches by Shawn Carpenter, an IDS analyst at Sandia Labs in New Mexico. Carpenter noticed unusual network activity in his logs and traced the hacks back to China. Poking around the C&C server he found numerous documents belonging to other targets of interest. Working with the FBI as a confidential informant over the next year he helped investigate a slew of attacks that the FBI dubbed Titan Rain.

Massive breaches have been recorded. The exfiltration of weapons systems design from the DIB, infiltration of DC based think tanks, breaches of law firms, and penetration of earth resource companies like Rio Tinto in Australia are all examples of nation-state actions.

For sophistication, nothing comes close to Operation Olympic Games (Stuxnet) that successfully disrupted Iran's nuclear refining program.

Countering nation-state actors requires the highest level of cyber defenses. Luckily, an organization that can effectively discover and disrupt or deny the activities of a well-funded nation-state cyber operation will have no problem countering attacks from other threat actors.

The technologies and methodologies for countering targeted attacks, be they from hackers, cyber criminals, or nation-states are evolving rapidly. Much of the methodologies have been independently derived at highly targeted organizations like Lockheed Martin, RSA (the security division of EMC), major banks, and new vendors.

Despite years of investment in multiple layers of security defenses, every organization is still wide open to targeted attacks. It is practically impossible to stop all attacks. Even Next Generation Firewalls, complete alerting and logging collected in a SIEM, and universal patch management and vulnerability discovery has proven to be ineffective against threat actors who are motivated, skilled and determined.

In an environment of constant unrelenting attacks, network packet capture, net flow recording and advanced security analytics are needed to discover the attack in progress and provide the intelligence to minimize the damage done. Advance knowledge of the reconnaissance phase, early probes of vulnerable systems, suspicious lateral movement, and attempted exfiltration can give the cyber defense team the time they need to thwart the attack and prepare for the follow-on attacks.

Security Analytics is the application of security intelligence to large data sets, usually of full packet captures or net flow data.

Security intelligence is any information that indicates an attack in progress or already successful. It may also include knowledge of attacker playbooks of the type iSIGHT Partners publishes.

Because every attacker has a vast set of tools available to him there are many more types of advanced attacks than attacker. Yet in the last three years some common methodologies have arisen. This category of attack, often called Advanced Persistent Threats (APTs) has become so common because it is so effective. The most critical differentiator from the malware, exploit, and random attacks of the last decade is the targeting. An attacker, be it cyber criminal, hacktivist, insider, or national spy agency, has pre-determined that your organization has information of use to them. It could be credit card information residing in Point of Sale terminals, as in the recent Target and Home Depot breaches. It could be designs of weapon systems, as in the exfiltration of F-35 Joint Strike Fighter data from the Defense Industrial Base. Or it could be the secret seeds to one-time password tokens, as in the successful attack against RSA, the security division of EMC.

To protect a network against a known piece of malware one simply updates AV systems with the latest signature databases or installs the latest patches. But to protect against a known attacker the requirements are much more involved.

Once an attacker has decided that your data is needed they continue to come back day after day. If your defenses are too strong, they attack your suppliers and trusted partners, such as an outside legal counsel. If you block them at the gateway, they come through an executive's laptop.

Security Analytics is big data science applied to full packet capture data, net flow, and event logs. The state of the art is to capture all traffic from each network segment, net flow data from routers and switches, and event information from firewalls and endpoints and subject it to complete analysis. The taps are passive in that they do not add a bump on the wire. The analytics is done offline. The overall technology is evolving rapidly with constant improvements that allows drilling down to the individual packet, looking at all traffic to get a big picture, and consuming external sources of intelligence such as Indicators of Compromise (IoC).

Scale, speed, and ability to apply security intelligence and correlating disparate events will be the determining factor in the success of SA tools.

Today an attack is run by human attackers sitting at remote computers. The defenders also need to constantly be surveilling their own networks to detect, deter, disrupt and block attacks.

Security Analytics has two components: a sensor deployed to a network segment for packet capture or net flow data generated by network devices such as routers, switches, and firewalls, and an analysis engine for the heavy lifting. The analysis engine parses and indexes all of the captured network traffic. An interface provides all of the analysis functions. A dashboard provides a high level view. It is when you start to mine the data that the intelligence magic is employed. Drill down to a single probe of the network over an unused port. Pivot to look at all other probes from the same source. Look at all similar activity. Determine when a reconnaissance phase shifted to a concerted attack. Find the queries to the Active Directory server. Follow those to the most recent machine touched by the domain admin's account (attackers can guess the domain admin just from activity logged in AD). Find the pass-the-hash attack against the database server. Slam the doors on the intruder.

(Pass-the-hash is an extraordinary weakness in Windows environments that must be explained. All Windows access is controlled through Active Directory, a simple directory of users that assigns privileges. The Domain Admin has the greatest privileges and can usually perform any activity on any machine, such as change policies, passwords, add or remove software, and of course read any file. When any administrator logs into any Windows machine she provides a password. A numerical hash of the password is created and looked up in a hash table in memory. If it is not in memory it is retrieved from Active Directory and compared to the hash of the password provided. If the hashes match the administrator is authenticated and allowed on. If the administrator then wants to login to another machine somewhere else on the network she does not have to re-input her password. The machine she is on "passes the hash" of her password to the next machine, which accepts it! An attacker who has gotten a foothold on the Active Directory server can see all login activity, make a few guesses about which machines the admin has recently visited, go to those machines, retrieve the hash, and use that to gain access to any machine on the network. In 2014, an Israeli startup, Aorato, created a defense against these pass-the-hash attacks and within months Microsoft had acquired it.[1] So it is likely that there will eventually be a solution for this major avenue of lethal lateral movement.)

There are three import features of a security analytics system. Scale, the ability to replay traffic, and an intuitive interface for data mining.

A single, fully saturated gigabit network, can generate 10.8 terabytes of data every day. An organization may need to retain 30-60 days of packet capture data to ensure that they have not been surveilled or compromised by advanced targeted attacks. Security analytics tools must be able to quickly replay hundreds of terabytes of data as new intelligence is available on threats. In practice, the scanning engine is updated, often weekly, whereupon the captured data is replayed and analyzed to catch new indicators of compromise or connections to known hostile IP addresses or domains.

Passing network traffic through an analysis engine is much like running a robust IDS tool in batch mode. But IDS has historically been a noisy generator of alerts requiring extensive tuning to reduce the volume. The alerts themselves create a data management issue that has been addressed by Security Information and Event Management (SIEM) tools. While modern SIEM tools have graphic interfaces that display long lists of alerts, stack ranked on "severity," they are little more that spreadsheets that require extraordinary amounts of time to address the thousands of high priority alerts generated. And, because IDS systems do not capture traffic, they typically indicate *something* happened without collecting the data to determine *what* happened.

Security analytics tools provide the ability to investigate network activity based on time-stamped data or other correlations. The ability to visualize data in terms of threats, sessions, protocols, streams, and files, makes network forensics possible and practical.

Security Analytics is evolving rapidly. First generation systems applied filters at the collection sensor to reduce the total amount of data being stored. Many so-called network recorders, designed to be able to replay sessions for troubleshooting or monitoring employee online behavior, evolved into threat analysis tools. Full packet capture for threat detection is relatively new. As the market grows for security analytics innovations will address these critical needs.

Realtime Security Analytics is needed to watch attacks while they are in progress. Experienced SA practitioners are becoming familiar with the deep dive data mining from today's SA tools but want to apply that same ability to understand packet flows in real or near real-time. Replaying legacy traffic against new intelligence will always be important, but as attacks become more automated the time required to react effectively will shrink.

Arbor Networks Pravail Security Analytics and RSA

Netwitness are two vendors that have created strong SA tools. Lancope is an Atlanta-based company that focuses on security analytics of Sflow data. Sqqrl is a startup created by former NSA analysts who have taken the NSA's big data analytics tools that the Software Assurance Directorate has made open source.

Automated response will be required to shun easily identified attack vectors or even completely anomalous behavior. While the industry has resisted connecting the plumbing between detection and protection devices the time is rapidly approaching when this will be required, especially for critical systems that can easily be disrupted by simple attacks such as manufacturing, critical infrastructure and medical systems.

Security analytics is the most powerful tool available to detect and counter today's APTs, which are characterized by identifiable phases of attack: recon, probing, payload delivery, command and control, and exfiltration. So far there is only one example of modern autonomous attack capability, dubbed Olympic Games or Stuxnet. Countering an attack that could be delivered and successfully executed in minutes instead of days will challenge all modern security defenses. Security Analytics is the precursor to future tools that will be designed to recognize and deflect autonomous attacks.

Security Analytics is one of the two fastest growing product categories in security. The other is sandboxing for advanced malware detection. As executables are delivered via email or direct download from websites they are "detonated" in a virtualized environment that is configured to detect malicious behavior like privilege escalation, command and control communication, or downloading of more malicious payloads. This is required because the most highly targeted attacks involve unique malware that is customized for the defender's systems. Often new zero-day vulnerabilities are exploited. Traditional AV would not identify these. Every organization will have to deploy some sort of security analytics coupled with network traffic monitoring and sandboxing. The largest IT departments in highly targeted environments, like banks and defense contractors, are already doing some sort of security analytics and advanced malware detection. The enterprise is hiring the talent now to be able to deploy and use security analytics. Smaller organizations will have to use managed service providers because they lack the staff. There will be standalone tools, cloud tools and capabilities built into network security platforms. Scale, speed and ability to apply security intelligence will be the determining factor in the success of these tools.

Security analytics is an emerging requirement in the ongoing arms race with threat actors. It has the advantage of applying to all threat actors. Vulnerability scanning and effective patching may have been the correct approach, even sufficient, back when the primary threat actors were hackers looking for vulnerable systems they could exploit. But sophisticated attackers need to be countered with sophisticated technology, people, and processes.

The Surveillance State represents the final threat actor. Beyond foreign state agencies, it turns out that one's own country may be spying on them. The difference between a foreign state actor and a local state actor is jurisdiction. One's own country may have the backing of law. The state can demand that an organization opens its networks to surveillance. Legal demands such as National Security Letters can be employed. These questionable instruments bind the recipients from even disclosing that they have received such a demand.

Legal issues aside, the remarkable capabilities of the NSA and GCHQ that have been revealed by the stream of revelations in

Snowden documents paint a picture of a truly sophisticated and determined digital adversary. The one advantage that the surveillance state has over any other attacker is access to the backbones of the service providers. They can install listening devices at the telephone company's central office (CO) and intercept all traffic. For decades it was assumed that it would be very difficult, for an attacker to intercept communications at the CO. An attacker would have to infiltrate the telecom provider, install equipment, and then maintain the presence of it. Telcoms have good physical security in their COs that would most likely prevent the attempts of cyber criminal gangs, or foreign nations from doing so.

In 2006 it was revealed by whistleblower Mark Klein that the San Francisco CO of AT&T had indeed been compromised by the NSA, which installed Narus packet capture gear in its San Francisco data center (Room 641A), which was capable of monitoring billions of bits of Internet traffic a second, including the playback of telephone calls routed on the Internet, in other words, surveillance on an unprecedented scale.

The activities of the Tailored Access Operation of the NSA, as revealed in the ANT catalog, paint a picture of astounding capabilities to infiltrate networks, install back doors on equipment, use close proximity to eavesdrop, and maintain persistence.

Threat management comes down to understanding the intent of an attacker and taking steps to thwart them. The most advanced practitioners of threat management are able to sort attacks into campaigns. Similar methods, tools, and other indicators, are associated with a campaign. The defenders can track a campaign over months and it is hoped continue to counter it as the attacker uses more and more sophisticated evolutions. The attackers may start with a simple probe of a network, or send a clumsily crafted email with a malicious attachment. As they fail to gain a foothold they "up their game." They may get better at crafting those emails, to the point where they appear to come from the CEO to the CFO asking for instructions on how to execute a wire transfer. They may use zero-day vulnerabilities and new exploits. Ultimately they could bribe or coerce the information they seek from an employee.

Most of the techniques outlined here require human monitoring and intervention to take action. As more organizations become better defended the attackers will start to automate their attacks. We have seen what this looks like; it's Stuxnet, a completely autonomous attack. Once Stuxnet was released it set in motion a series of actions that accomplished a goal.

Autonomous attacks will require automated defense to thwart. Few organizations are ready to implement automated defense. They have several years to prepare before they will be necessary.

CHAPTER EIGHTEEN

Conclusion

Perhaps the risks have not been adequately illuminated in this book. For a business, university, or minor government agency, the risk of debilitating cyber attack, like that against Sony Entertainment, only more severe, could be as high as destruction of that business, revamping of management, and a scramble to recover. In the end, recovery is usually possible. The reason that so much hand wringing is applied to the risks of cyber attack against critical infrastructure is that much of the potential damage is irreversible, in particular the deaths of hospital patients, factory workers, or the masses in the event of a catastrophic disabling of power, oil and gas, and communication. Indeed, lives will be lost but life will go on. The recovery time will be proportionate to the severity and success of the attack.

In military affairs the consequences cascade. Something as simple as tampering with communications could lead to the loss of a battle. A full-on cyberwar that included successful attacks against ISR, C&C, and weapons platforms could mean a strategic advantage for the enemy. In other words, the loss of a battle could change the balance of power.

Yes it works both ways. The DoD could employ cyber attacks to gain the advantage in future wars. But other than glimmers of the NSA's capabilities provided by leaks to the press (many from the White House), we do not have the resources to evaluate the US's ability to wage the types of attacks described in this book or how those tactics are incorporated in battle plans, both tactical and strategic. We do know, thanks to the numerous breaches and failures of military operations and weapons systems, that the US is woefully unprepared to counter theater cyberwar. In the meantime, documents that address the cyber domain do not call for attacks against adversary C&C, ISR, and weapons platforms. They typically address the potential for attacking critical infrastructure of a country or defending critical infrastructure of the United States.

The final defense for a commercial operation or small government agency is recovery. Rebuild computers with new images. Deploy new defenses. Restore data from backup. Get email working again. That process is always more expensive than deploying the appropriate defenses beforehand would have been. In military affairs that process may not be an option. Losing battles leads to losing wars.

The proscriptive measures proposed here are not likely to ever be deployed in time. They are a roadmap to recovery after the loss. Building the cyber defenses needed for the DoD to continue to be an effective means of projecting force is just too expensive politically and in national treasure.

The last best hope is that a future attack is demonstrative of the lack of cyber preparedness on the part of the US military, yet does not change the strategic balance. The loss of Taiwan, or the defeat of a fleet in the contested South China Sea, or loss of yet another Eastern European country to Russia, will be disastrous. But it will give us fair warning. Even then, the ensuing political theater, hastily construed legislation and Executive Orders that are the likely fallout, will hardly address the core issues exposed by the loss.

ACKNOWLEDGEMENTS

This project could only have come to fruition with the assistance of a community of researchers, experts, editors, and supporters. Chief in the supporter category is my wife, Karen Ethier, who encourages me in all my ventures, be they technology startups, investments in technology startups, launching a consulting practice, going back to school, or writing a book.

As I wrote my first book, *Surviving Cyberwar*, I quickly realized that I was recording one of the first histories of cyber conflict and that my amateur love of military history would probably be identified as just that: amateur. I began a search for a university that could backfill not only my knowledge of military history but also provide the underpinnings of historiography and the numerous schools of academic thought associated with strategic studies and military history. I found that in the *War in the Modern World* program at King's College, London. When I first enrolled cyberwar was not a topic covered by any of the professors. By the time I graduated in 2014 there were three books on cyberwar penned by King's researchers and Thomas Rid had taken several Phd candidates under his wing with strong backgrounds in IT security. I have my dissertation adviser, David Betz, to thank for his guidance throughout the process and for what must have been a daunting task: reading my dissertation.

Along the way, I received support from many people. Dr. Ken Morgan in Perth kept me supplied with daily updates clipped from newsletters, Congressional announcements, and his own thoughts. This constant feed started when I was researching my dissertation topic and continued through to the conversion of that dissertation to this book. Even today he continues his daily ritual of walking to the sea, sitting with his morning coffee and enlivening my evenings by sending me cybersecurity news of tomorrow from his iPad.

I want to thank Lt. Colonel (ret) Bill Hagestad of Red Dragon Rising for his assistance along the way. He is fluent in Chinese and an expert on Chinese cyber affairs. He responds immediately if I have need of a quick translation of a Chinese policy or news item. His Twitter feed @RedDragon1949 is a comprehensive stream of Chinese cyber news. I am deeply in debt for his review at the last minute of the first two chapters of this book.

Special thanks to Michael Warner, the CIA historian assigned to US Cybercom, for providing a copy of *Stand Up and Fight! The Creation of US Security Organizations, 1942-2005,* a document from the US Military Academy which includes his history of US Cybercom.

Allen Bernard provided guidance on rewriting the dissertation into a book.

As always, Joe Ponepinto provided the first eyes to read and edit my manuscript. He is my mentor and writing coach. He can't resist fact checking along the way which is of tremendous help. His team at Woodward Press provided coordination and guidance on the cover design. And finally, I thank Courtney Feldman, the best copy editor I could have, for her quick and accurate turnaround of my completed manuscript. I could not have made my deadline without her.

Cover Credits
Cover Design: Martin Butler
Author Photo: Karen Ethier

NOTES

To ease the reader's task of looking up citations these notes contain enough information to find the original sources. Where an article is easily found by searching on the text, no URL is provided. These notes can also be found at ITH-press.com and links are provided there.

CHAPTER TWO

1. As this book goes to press the Defense Authorization Act before Congress includes "a new initiative to enable the services to begin evaluating all major weapons systems for cyber vulnerabilities." NATIONAL DEFENSE AUTHORIZATION ACT FOR FISCAL YEAR 2016
(Senate - June 03, 2015) https://www.congress.gov/congressional-record/2015/06/03/senate-section/article/s3642-1/

2. Details of Archie Clemins' story of the Blue Ridge and his deployment of two carrier battle groups towards the Taiwan Straits are from notes taken during a conversation with Admiral Clemins February 18, 2015.

3. Mark Lenci provided background information on the Blue Ridge story. Notes from a conversation February, 2015.

4. The irony of a PowerPoint presentation being the killer app that

sold the Joint Chiefs cannot pass unremarked. PowerPoint presentations have become the bane of military planning operations. During the protracted war in Iraq an Air Force sortie could not launch until the obligatory briefing fueled by PowerPoint presentations. A system was devised that would take up-to-date elements of weather, geography, and terminology and centralize them in Colorado Springs so that everywhere in the world every PowerPoint would be updated with the current data and graphics. Military planners have become masters of PowerPoint. The pushback against the tyranny of bullet points has grown to the point where the newly appointed Secretary of Defense, Ashton Carter, barred PowerPoint from his briefing with "30 high-ranking military commanders and diplomats" at a meeting he called in Kuwait for February, 2015. Whitlock, Kevin "Carter summons U.S. military commanders, diplomats to Kuwait" Washington Post, February 22, 2015.

5. Arthur S. Ding p. 213 Globalization and Security Relations across the Taiwan Strait: In the shadow of China. Routledge, Nov 27, 2014

CHAPTER THREE

1. I took time out from writing *There Will Be Cyberwar* to contribute the first chapter, on the history of cyber warfare, to this collection edited by James A. Greene: *Cyber Warfare: A Multidisciplinary Analysis* (Routledge, May 2015)

2. The NATO Cooperative Cyber Defense Centre of Excellence was expanded to today's position of thought leadership after the Russian attacks on Estonia of 2007. It holds conferences every

year and has published important documents like the Tallinn Manual on the International Law Applicable to Cyber Warfare, edited by Michael N. Schmitt. They have also published a taxonomy of cyber terms at https://ccdcoe.org/cyber-definitions.html

3. Austrian Cybersecurity Strategy, Vienna, 2003 PDF https://www.bka.gv.at/DocView.axd

4. Shane Harris has written one of the more compelling books on cyberwar although his definition may be viewed by many as overly broad. Using phony cell phone messages may be relegated to the part of military ruse. @War: The Rise of the Military-Internet Complex (Eamon Dolan/Houghton Mifflin Harcourt, November 11, 2014)

5. Adrian Chen has written an excellent piece for *The New York Times* on the Russian troll farm in St. Petersburg. June 2, 2015 http://www.nytimes.com/2015/06/07/magazine/the-agency.html

6. Freedom House: China's growing army of paid internet commentators https://freedomhouse.org/blog/china's-growing-army-paid-internet-commentators

7. TelesurTV, UK to Create Cyber Warfare Agency February 2, 2015 http://www.telesurtv.net/english/news/UK-to-Create-Cyber-Warfare-Agency-20150201-0017.html

8. In 2008 a fraud ring was uncovered that had embedded chips in Point of Sale terminals manufactured in China. Gorman, Siobhan "Fraud Ring Funnels Data From Cards to Pakistan" *Wall*

Street Journal 11 October 2008 http://online.wsj.com/news/
articles/SB122366999999723871

9. Poulson, Kevin "Wireless hacking bust in Michigan
Warparking" The Register 13 Nov 2003 http://
www.theregister.co.uk/2003/11/13/
wireless_hacking_bust_in_michigan/

10. The fact that the breach at TJX was accomplished in such a
similar way to that of Lowes four years before speaks volumes
about the the ability of retailers to learn from anything but their
own mistakes. Savvas, Antony, "TJX hack the biggest in history"
Computer Weekly 02 April 2007 http://
www.computerweekly.com/news/2240080607/TJX-hack-the-
biggest-in-history

11. Krebs, Brian. Target Hackers Broke in Via HVAC Company
http://krebsonsecurity.com/2014/02/target-hackers-broke-in-
via-hvac-company/

12. Full disclosure: I assisted Gemalto in creating the algorithm for
computing the data breach index numbers. Gemalto Findings,
Data Breach Level Index 2014 http://breachlevelindex.com/pdf/
Breach-Level-Index-Annual-Report-2014.pdf   [Note: Just after
publishing its Breach Level Index Report, Gemalto was identified
in Snowden documents. It too had suffered a breach, perhaps one
of the most damaging ever, from the NSA. The Snowden
documents revealed that the NSA working with GCHQ had
breached Gemalto and stolen as many as 60 million encryption
keys that are embedded in the SIM microchips installed in every
cell phone in the world.]

13. Perlroth, Nicole. Hackers in China Attacked The Times for Last 4 Months, *The New York Times* January 30, 2013 http://www.nytimes.com/2013/01/31/technology/chinese-hackers-infiltrate-new-york-times-computers.html

14. U.S.-Canada Power System Outage Task Force: Final Report on the August 14, 2003 Blackout in the United States and Canada. http://energy.gov/sites/prod/files/oeprod/DocumentsandMedia/BlackoutFinal-Web.pdf

15. Shodan map of industrial control systems connected to the Internet. https://icsmap.shodan.io/

16. Robert M. Lee, Michael J. Assante, and Tim Conway. German Steel Mill Cyber Attack. SANS ICS Defense Use Case (DUC), December 30, 2014 https://ics.sans.org/media/ICS-CPPE-case-Study-2-German-Steelworks_Facility.pdf

17. Most of the major industry analyst firms track the size of the overall IT security market. Gartner pegs the space at $62 Billion in 2012 and set to grow 8.7 Percent in 2013. No market research firm has ever predicted accurately the true growth of the space which has grown 17 fold in ten years. IT-Harvest predicts that post-Snowden the space will grow at 24% annually. Gartner press release "Gartner Says Worldwide Security Market to Grow 8.7 Percent in 2013" 11 June 2013 http://www.gartner.com/newsroom/id/2512215

18. Gorman, Siobhan and Barnes, Julian E. "Iranian Hacking to

Test NSA Nominee Michael Rogers Infiltration of Navy Computer Network More Extensive Than Previously Thought" The Wall Street Journal 18 February 2014 http://online.wsj.com/news/articles/SB10001424052702304899704579389402826681452

19. Zorabedian, John "SophosLabs: Android malware intercepts SMS messages to steal mobile banking codes" 5 February 2014 http://blogs.sophos.com/2014/02/05/sophoslabs-android-malware-intercepts-sms-messages-to-steal-banking-info/

20. Gorman, Siobhan Cole, August and Dreazen, Yochi "Computer Spies Breach Fighter-Jet Project" Wall Street Journal 21 April 2009 http://online.wsj.com/news/articles/SB124027491029837401

21. One of the more important articles supporting the thesis of this book. Nakashima, Ellen "Confidential report lists U.S. weapons system designs compromised by Chinese cyberspies" Washington Post 27 May 2013
22. Thornburgh, Nathan. The Invasion of the Chinese Cyberspies An exclusive look at how the hackers called TITAN RAIN are stealing U.S. secrets *Time Magazine*, Monday, Aug. 29, 2005 You can read the full story of Shawn Carpenter and Sandia in *Surviving Cyberwar*.

23. Sevastopulo, Demetri "Chinese hacked into Pentagon" Financial Times 3 September 2007 http://www.ft.com/intl/cms/s/0/9dba9ba2-5a3b-11dc-9bcd-0000779fd2ac.html

24. Singer, P.W. Wired for War: The Robotics Revolution and Conflict in the 21st Century (Penguin Press 2009) p. 201

25. Nakashima, Ellen. "Cyber-intruder sparks massive federal response — and debate over dealing with threats" Washington Post 8 December 2011 http://www.washingtonpost.com/national/national-security/cyber-intruder-sparks-response-debate/2011/12/06/gIQAxLuFgO_story.html

26. Still the most important writing on the DoD's wake up call. Lynn, William J. III "Defending a New Domain: The Pentagon's Cyberstrategy" Foreign Affairs, Vol. 89, No. 5 (September/October 2010), pp. 97-108

27. F-Secure is an endpoint protection vendor whose reputation has grown in post-Snowden days thanks to it's outspoken Chief Research Officer Mikko Hypponen. Follow him on Twitter @mikko "F-Secure classification of Agent.btz worm" http://www.f-secure.com/v-descs/worm_w32_agent_btz.shtml

28. Berg, Barry "Army CIO sets sights on improved data sharing" Government Computing News 10 August 2009 http://gcn.com/articles/2009/08/10/gcn-interview-sorenson-army-cio.aspx

29. Department of Defense Fiscal Year(FY) 2011 IT President's Budget Request March 2010 as found at http://www.scribd.com/doc/56044639/Airforce-Overview-Pb2011

30. Alexander, David. "Pentagon flash drive ban has many exceptions" Reuters 22 June 2013 http://www.reuters.com/article/2013/06/22/us-usa-security-pentagon-idUSBRE95L06520130622?

31. I follow the convention of naming a person based on his/her identity at the time. Bradley Manning has since changed her name to Chelsea Manning. Leigh, David. "How 250,000 US embassy cables were leaked from a fake Lady Gaga CD to a thumb drive that is a pocket-sized bombshell – the biggest intelligence leak in history" The Guardian 28 November 2010 http://www.theguardian.com/world/2010/nov/28/how-us-embassy-cables-leaked

32. Greenberg, Andy. "NSA Implementing 'Two-Person' Rule To Stop The Next Edward Snowden" Forbes 18 June 2013 http://www.forbes.com/sites/andygreenberg/2013/06/18/nsa-director-says-agency-implementing-two-person-rule-to-stop-the-next-edward-snowden/

33. Sanger, David E. "N.S.A. Forces Out Civilian Employee With Snowden Tie" New York Times 13 February 2014 http://www.nytimes.com/2014/02/14/us/politics/nsa-fires-civilian-employee-tied-to-snowden-leaks.html

34. Gorman, Siobhan and Barnes, Julian E. "Iranian Hacking to Test NSA Nominee Michael Rogers Infiltration of Navy Computer Network More Extensive Than Previously Thought" The Wall Street Journal 18 February 2014 http://online.wsj.com/news/articles/SB10001424052702304899704579389402826681452

35. Alberts, David S. and Hayes, Richard E. Power to the Edge: Command and Control in the Information Age DoD Command and Control Research Program publication 2003

36. DARPA Broad Agency Announcement for Communications in

Contested Environments dated 20 December 2013 DARPA-
BAA-14-02_Communications_in_Contested_Environments_(C2
E).pdf

37. The DoD QDRs are excellent historical documents that are
supposed to be forward looking but often merely encapsulate
current military thinking. Department of Defense Quadrennial
Defense Review http://www.defense.gov/pubs/
2014_Quadrennial_Defense_Review.pdf

CHAPTER FOUR

1.   To be exact Metcalf's law is an expression of the number of
unique connections in a fully meshed network: $n(n - 1)/2$. The
more devices connected to a network the more "value."

2. Microsoft: Life in the Digital Cross Hairs. Multimedia report
http://www.microsoft.com/security/sdl/story/

3. Note the date of Bill Gates' "wake up call", January 2002, well
before the Pentagon had their moment in 2007-8. Gates, Bill
"Trustworthy Computing" Microsoft memo 15 January 2002
http://www.microsoft.com/en-us/news/features/2012/jan12/
gatesmemo.aspx

4. I write more about this tendency to not build security in from
the beginning here: Stiennon, Richard "Six security dangers Web
startups should know and how to counter them" GigaOm report, 6
March 2012 http://research.gigaom.com/report/six-security-
dangers-web-startups-should-know-and-how-to-counter-them/

5. Gartner press release "Gartner Says Worldwide Security Market to Grow 8.7 Percent in 2013" 11 June 2013 http://www.gartner.com/newsroom/id/2512215

CHAPTER FIVE

1. Ledbetter, James *Starving to Death on $200 Million: The Short, Absurd Life of The Industry Standard* p.3 (PublicAffairs; 1st edition, January 2003)

2. Remarks by Chairman Alan Greenspan At the Annual Dinner and Francis Boyer Lecture of The American Enterprise Institute for Public Policy Research, Washington, D.C. December 5, 1996 http://www.federalreserve.gov/boarddocs/speeches/19961205.htm

CHAPTER SIX

1.   Liaropolous, Andrew N. "Revolutions in Warfare: Theoretical Paradigms and Historical Evidence–The Napoleonic and First World War Revolutions in Military Affairs" p. 364 The Journal of Military History 70 (April 2006): 363–84

2. Owens, William A. Lifting the Fog of War (Farrar, Straus, and Giroux, 2000) p. 80-82

3. Stiennon, Richard Surviving Cyberwar (Government Institutes, 2010) p. 16-17

4. Thomas, Timothy L. Decoding the Virtual Dragon (Foreign

Military Studies Office, Fort Leavenworth, KS, 2007) p. 333

5. US Army War College REVOLUTION IN MILITARY AFFAIRS: A SELECTED BIBLIOGRAPHY. US Army War College Library, May 1996

6. Krepinevich, Andrew F. "Calvary to Computer, The Pattern of Military Revolutions," The National Interest. Fall 1994, 30.

7. Rosen, Stephen P. "The Impact of the Office of Net Assessment on the American Military in the Matter of the Revolution in Military Affairs" Journal of Strategic Studies, 33:4 469-482, 20 Aug 2010 p. 470

8. ibid p. 482

CHAPTER SEVEN

1. Cebrowski, Arthur K. and Garstka, John J. "Network-Centric Warfare: Its Origin and Future" Proceedings January 1998 http://mattcegelske.com/wp-content/uploads/2012/04/ncw_origin_future.pdf

2. ibid

3. NIST, "The History of Worms" http://csrc.nist.gov/publications/nistir/threats/subsubsection3_3_2_1.html

4. Cebrowski, Arthur K. and Garstka, John J. p. 6

5. Singer, p 191 Singer, P.W. *Wired for War: The Robotics Revolution and Conflict in the 21st Century* (Penguin Press 2009)

6. Blaker, John R. *Transforming Military Force: The Legacy of Arthur Cebrowski and Network Centric Warfare* (Praeger Security International, 2007) p. 119

7. Video: Pentagon briefing November 27, 2001 Cebrowski "Director of Force Transformation" CSPAN http://www.c-span.org/video/?167476-1/operations-afghanistan

8. Video: AIAA Conference, Washington, DC February 19, 2002 "Military Readiness and National Security" http://www.c-span.org/video/?168746-4/military-readiness-national-security

9. Everstine, Brian "Why the Air Force wants to keep Global Hawks and retire U-2s" *Air Force Times* Mar. 5, 2014 http://archive.airforcetimes.com/article/20140305/NEWS04/303050029/Why-Air-Force-wants-keep-Global-Hawks-retire-U-2s

10. Video: US Chamber of Commerce December 3, 2003 event in Washington, DC. "Security Planning and Military Transformation" http://www.c-span.org/video/?179350-1/security-planning-military-transformation

11. Singer   p. 200

12. Peters, Ralph. "The Future of Armored Warfare" Parameters, Autumn 1997, pp. 50-59. http://strategicstudiesinstitute.army.mil/pubs/parameters/Articles/

97autumn/peters.htm

13. Biddle, Stephen "AFGHANISTAN AND THE FUTURE OF WARFARE: IMPLICATIONS FOR ARMY AND DEFENSE POLICY" November 2002 Strategic Studies Institute, U.S. Army War College http://www.au.af.mil/au/awc/awcgate/ssi/afghan.pdf

14. Defense.org "CNO: Next-Generation Navy Fighter Might Not Need Stealth" Feb. 14, 2015 http://defensetech.org/2015/02/05/cno-next-generation-navy-fighter-might-not-need-stealth/#ixzz3R5IiZLCU

CHAPTER EIGHT

1. Adams, James "Virtual Defense" Foreign Affairs, May/June 2001 Stable URL: http://www.jstor.org/stable/20050154

2. Warner, Michael, "US Cyber Command's Road to Full Operational Capability" Stand Up and Fight! The Creation of US Security Organizations, 1942-2005 ed. Seidule , Ty, Whitt, Jacqueline (United States Military Academy, 2013 Under Review For Publication, AUSA Press) Just made available April, 2015 here: http://www.strategicstudiesinstitute.army.mil/pubs/display.cfm?pubID=1264

3. Joint Chiefs of Staff, The National Strategy of the USA, 2004 http://www.defense.gov/news/mar2005/d20050318nms.pdf

4. Air Force Cyber Letter http://www.24af.af.mil/shared/media/document/AFD-111003-051.pdf

5. Richard Bejtlich is the author of the Tao Security blog, one of the earliest and longest lasting security blogs. He is currently Chief Security Strategist at FireEye, Inc.. Bejtlich, Richard. "Whither Air Force Cyber?" http://taosecurity.blogspot.com/2008/10/whither-air-force-cyber.html 9 October 2008

6. IDC Self Synchronization. Navy 10th fleet. http://www.idcsync.org/about/fltcybercom-c10f

7. Warner, p. 35

8. Warner, p. 36

9. IA Newsletter "US Cyber Command is Activated" IANewsletter Vol 12 Number 3 Summer 2010 http://www.surviac.wpafb.af.mil/csiac/download/Vol13_No3.pdf#page=15

10. US Cyber Command Fact Sheet http://www.defense.gov/home/features/2010/0410_cybersec/docs/CYberFactSheet%20UPDATED%20replaces%20May%2021%20Fact%20Sheet.pdf

11. Alexander, Keith B. STATEMENT OF GENERAL KEITH B. ALEXANDER COMMANDER UNITED STATES CYBER COMMAND BEFORE THE SENATE COMMITTEE ON ARMED SERVICES 12 MARCH 2013

12. Reed, John. "Cyber Command fielding 13 "offensive" cyber deterrence units" Foreign Policy, 12 March 2013 http://complex.foreignpolicy.com/posts/2013/03/12/us_cyber_command_developing_13_offensive_cyber_deterrence

_units

13. NextGov Need a Job? Cyber Command Is Halfway Full http://www.nextgov.com/cybersecurity/2015/02/need-job-cyber-command-halfway-full/104817/

14. Senate Intelligence and Military Nominations. C-Span video11 March 2014 http://www.c-span.org/video/?318215-1/confirmation-hearing-national-security-nominees

CHAPTER NINE

1. Black Budget *Washington Post* http://www.washingtonpost.com/wp-srv/special/national/black-budget/

2. Cryptome tally of Snowden documents published to-date http://cryptome.org/2013/11/snowden-tally.htm

3. Hutchins, Eric M., Cloppert, Michael J., Amin, Rohan M. "Intelligence-Driven Computer Network Defense Informed by Analysis of Adversary Campaigns and Intrusion Kill Chains" Lockheed Martin paper http://www.lockheedmartin.com/content/dam/lockheed/data/corporate/documents/LM-White-Paper-Intel-Driven-Defense.pdf

4. Mandiant "APT1: Exposing One of China's Cyber Espionage Units" Mandiant publication http://intelreport.mandiant.com/Mandiant_APT1_Report.pdf

5. Allen, Jonathan. "NSA to cut system administrators by 90 percent to limit data access" Reuters 8 August 2013

6. Kirschbaum, Erik. "Snowden says NSA engages in industrial espionage: TV" Reuters 26 January 2014

7. Thomson, Iain, "Schneier: NSA snooping tactics will be copied by criminals in 3 to 5 years" *The Register* 26 Feb 2014 http://www.theregister.co.uk/2014/02/26/nsa_snooping_tactics_will_be_copied_by_criminals_in_35_years/

8. Stiennon, Richard "The Incredible Power of XKeyscore" securitycurrent 30 December 2013, http://www.securitycurrent.com/en/writers/richard-stiennon/the-incredible-power-of-xkeyscore

9. Ball, James. "Angry Birds and 'leaky' phone apps targeted by NSA and GCHQ for user data" The Guardian, 28 January 2014 http://www.theguardian.com/world/2014/jan/27/nsa-gchq-smartphone-app-angry-birds-personal-data

10. Peterson, Andrea "Look at this amazing drawing the NSA made for its hacking system" *The Washington Post* December 30, 2013

11. Appelbaum, Jacob, Horchert, Judith, Stöcker, Christian. "Shopping for Spy Gear: Catalog Advertises NSA Toolbox" *Spiegel Online* 29 December 2013 http://www.spiegel.de/international/world/catalog-reveals-nsa-has-back-doors-for-numerous-devices-a-940994.html

12. Page 1 of the NSA ANT Catalog hosted by Electronic Frontier Foundation (EFF) https://www.eff.org/document/20131230-appelbaum-nsa-ant-catalog

13. ibid p. 2

14. ibid p. 3

15. ibid p. 5

16. Schneier, Bruce "HEADWATER: NSA Exploit of the Day" Schneier on Security 14 January 2014 https://www.schneier.com/blog/archives/2014/01/headwater_nsa_e.html

17. NSA ANT Catalog p. 42

18. Bridges, Peter George Kennan Reminisces About Moscow in 1933–1937, *Diplomacy & Statecraft*, 2006 17:2, 283-293

19. NSA ANT Catalog p. 13

20. Montlake, Simon. "U.S. Congress Flags China's Huawei, ZTE As Security Threats" Forbes 10 August 2012 http://www.forbes.com/sites/simonmontlake/2012/10/08/u-s-congress-flags-chinas-huawei-zte-as-security-threats/

21. NSA ANT Catalog p. 24

22. Sanger, David E. "Obama Order Sped Up Wave of Cyberattacks Against Iran" *The New York Times* 1 June 2012 http://www.nytimes.com/2012/06/01/world/middleeast/obama-

ordered-wave-of-cyberattacks-against-iran.html

23. Nakashima, Ellen. "Stuxnet was work of U.S. and Israeli experts, officials say" *Washington Post* 1 June 2012. http://www.washingtonpost.com/world/national-security/stuxnet-was-work-of-us-and-israeli-experts-officials-say/2012/06/01/gJQAlnEy6U_story.html

24. Gjelten, Tom. "Security Expert: U.S. 'Leading Force' Behind Stuxnet" NPR 26 September 2011 http://www.npr.org/2011/09/26/140789306/security-expert-u-s-leading-force-behind-stuxnet

25. Despite the headline of this article, from the Snowden interviews one could interpret that he was merely repeating what had been revealed by Sanger, et. al., not confirming from his insider knowledge. JTA, "Snowden says Israel, U.S. created Stuxnet virus that attacked Iran" Haaretz 19 July 2013 http://www.haaretz.com/news/diplomacy-defense/1.534728

26. CBS "Iran Confirms Stuxnet Worm Halted Centrifuges" http://www.cbsnews.com/news/iran-confirms-stuxnet-worm-halted-centrifuges/

27. Microsoft Security Bulletin MS10-046 - Critical http://technet.microsoft.com/en-us/security/bulletin/MS10-046

28. Moore, David et al "The Spread of the Sapphire/Slammer Worm" The Cooperative Association for Internet Data Analysis http://www.caida.org/publications/papers/2003/sapphire/sapphire.html

29. Kehoe, Brendan P. "Zen and the Art of the Internet: A Beginner's Guide to the Internet, First Edition, January 1992 http://www.cs.indiana.edu/docproject/zen/zen-1.0_10.html#SEC91

30. Naraine, Ryan "Stuxnet attackers used 4 Windows zero-day exploits" ZDNET 14 September 2010 http://www.zdnet.com/blog/security/stuxnet-attackers-used-4-windows-zero-day-exploits/7347

31. Raiu, Costin. "Stuxnet signed certificates frequently asked questions" Securelist 21 July 2010 http://www.securelist.com/en/blog2236Stuxnet_signed_certificates_frequently_asked_questions

CHAPTER TEN

1. Senate Report 112–167 INQUIRY INTO COUNTERFEIT ELECTRONIC PARTS IN THE DEPARTMENT OF DEFENSE SUPPLY CHAIN 21 May 2012

2. Charette, Robert N. "F-35 Program Continues to Struggle with Software " *IEEE Spectrum* 19 September 2012 http://spectrum.ieee.org/riskfactor/aerospace/military/f35-program-continues-to-struggle-with-software

3. DARPA Trusted Integrated Circuits (TRUST) http://www.darpa.mil/Our_Work/MTO/Programs/Trusted_Integrated_Circuits_%28TRUST%29.aspx

4. J. Michael Gilmore DOT&E FY2014 Annual Report Director Operational Test & Evaluation http://www.dote.osd.mil/pub/ reports/FY2014/pdf/other/2014cybersecurity.pdf

5. Hersh, Seymour M. "Annals of National Security The Online Threat Should we be worried about a cyber war?" New Yorker 1 November 2010 http://www.newyorker.com/reporting/ 2010/11/01/101101fa_fact_hersh

6. OASIS Message to Technical Committee 1 October 2010 https://lists.oasis-open.org/archives/tc-announce/201010/ msg00000.html

7. Hagen, Christian and Sorenson, Jeff. "Delivering Military Software Affordably" Defense AT&L Magazine March-April 2013

8. GAO Testimony Before the Subcommittee on Tactical Air and Land Forces, Committee on Armed Services, House of Representatives. Statement of Michael J. Sullivan, Director Acquisition and Sourcing Management 20 March 2012   p. 9

9. Cigital Federal. Addressing Software Security in the Federal Acquisition Process p. 7 14 January 2011 white paper available at http://www.cigital.com/whitepapers/dl/ Addressing_Software_Assurance_in_the_Federal_Acquisition_P rocess.pdf

10. ibid

11. Microsoft: Life in the Digital Cross Hairs. Multimedia report

http://www.microsoft.com/security/sdl/story/

12. Gates, Bill "Trustworthy Computing" Microsoft memo15 January 2002 http://www.microsoft.com/en-us/news/features/2012/jan12/gatesmemo.aspx

13. Microsoft Security Advisory (2934088) "Vulnerability in Internet Explorer Could Allow Remote Code Execution" http://technet.microsoft.com/en-us/security/advisory/2934088 Published: Wednesday, February 19, 2014

14. Lynn, William J. III "Defending a New Domain: The Pentagon's Cyberstrategy" *Foreign Affairs*, Vol. 89, No. 5 (September/October 2010), pp. 97-108

15. Kissel, Richard. "Security Considerations in the System Development Life Cycle" NIST Special Publication 800-64 Revision 2, October 2008

CHAPTER ELEVEN

1. Gorman, Siobhan Cole, August and Dreazen, Yochi "Insurgents Hack U.S. Drones: $26 Software Is Used to Breach Key Weapons in Iraq; Iranian Backing Suspected" Wall Street Journal 17 December 2009 http://online.wsj.com/news/articles/SB126102247889095011

2. Majumdar, Dave "Iran's captured RQ-170: How bad is the damage?" Air Force Times 9 December 2011 http://www.airforcetimes.com/article/20111209/NEWS/112090311/

Iran-s-captured-RQ-170-How-bad-is-the-damage-

3. PressTV report "Iran releases decoded footage obtained from captured US drone" http://www.presstv.ir/detail/2013/02/07/287743/iran-releases-decoded-video-from-us-drone/

4. Templeton, Graham. "Hackers hijack a super yacht with simple GPS spoofing, and planes could be next" ExtremeTech 29 July 2013 http://www.extremetech.com/extreme/162462-hackers-hijack-a-super-yacht-with-simple-gps-spoofing-and-planes-could-be-next

5. Bozorgmehr, Shirzad "Iran says it captured 'enemy drone'" CNN 23 February 2013 http://www.cnn.com/2013/02/23/world/meast/iran-drone/index.html

6. Kreps, Sarah and Zenko, Micah "The Next Drone Wars." Foreign Affairs. February 12, 2014. http://www.foreignaffairs.com/articles/140746/sarah-kreps-and-micah-zenko/the-next-drone-wars

7. Rawnsley, Adam. "North Korean Jammer Forces Down U.S. Spy Plane" Wired 12 September 2011 http://www.wired.com/dangerroom/2011/09/north-korean-jammer-forces-down-u-s-spy-plane/

8. IETF on STDMA http://www.ietf.org/mail-archive/web/16ng/current/pdfMPHfh65EKH.pdf

9. Almeida, Rob. "Iranian Tanker Hacks AIS to Disguise Itself Off

Singapore" GCaptain 25 October 2013 http://gcaptain.com/
iranian-tanker-hacks-disguise/

10. Wilhoit, Kyle and Balduzzi, Marco. "Vulnerabilities Discovered
in Global Vessel Tracking Systems" Trend Micro http://
blog.trendmicro.com/trendlabs-security-intelligence/
vulnerabilities-discovered-in-global-vessel-tracking-systems/

11. CNS Systems "An STDMA Communications System for the U.S.
Navy1997" http://www.cnssys.com/FASSTER.php

12. This report of the successful integration of commercial AIS into
the Global Hawk drones was published in December, 2008: "The
team's accomplishments included performing more than 1,000
hours of flight operations over an 18-month period,
troubleshooting issues with the communications system,
integrating the automatic identification system into the aircraft so
it can be used in civilian air space, conducting tests with the ocean
surveillance initiative, and developing tactics and guidelines for
unmanned patrol systems." *Defense Industry Daily* http://
www.defenseindustrydaily.com/global-hawk-uav-prepares-for-
maritime-role-updated-01218/

CHAPTER TWELVE

1. Butler, Amy. "Neighborhood Watch: U.S. Air Force to deploy
'taskable" intel sats to spy in GEO belt" *Aviation Week & Space
Technology* 3 March 2014 p. 22

2. Morring, Frank Jr. "Satellite Cyber: Hybrid systems bring satellite operators new security challenges" *Aviation Week & Space Technology* 17 March 2014 p. 30

3. Hennigan, W.J. "Jamming the enemy: In the shadowy world of electronic warfare, there are no deadly missiles and fiery blasts, but the effect is the same" Los Angeles Times, 14 March 2014 http://articles.latimes.com/2014/mar/14/business/la-fi-electronic-warfare-20140314

CHAPTER THIRTEEN

1. Fulghum, David A. "When is Cyberattack Not EW? Perhaps Never." Aviation Week & Space Technology, 28 March 2012

2. Riedel, Bruce "Lessons of the Syrian Reactor" The National Interest, May-June 2013 http://nationalinterest.org/article/lessons-the-syrian-reactor-8380

3. The story of Israel 'injecting code" into Russian built radar systems is one of very few examples ever cited of military cyber attack, and is sparsely reported with David Fulghum, an editor at AW&ST, being practically the only source. Fulghum, David A. "Why Syria's Air Defenses Failed to Detect Israelis" Aviation Week & Space Technology 3 October 2007

4. Hennigan, W.J. "Jamming the enemy: In the shadowy world of electronic warfare, there are no deadly missiles and fiery blasts, but the effect is the same" Los Angeles Times, 14 March 2014 http://articles.latimes.com/2014/mar/14/business/la-fi-electronic-warfare-20140314

5. Schmitt, Eric and Shanker, Thom. "U.S. Debated Cyberwarfare in Attack Plan on Libya" New York Times, 17 October 2011 http://www.nytimes.com/2011/10/18/world/africa/cyber-warfare-against-libya-was-debated-by-us.html

6. Fulghum, David A. "When is Cyberattack Not EW? Perhaps Never." Aviation Week & Space Technology, 28 March 2012

CHAPTER FOURTEEN

1. Department of Defense Strategy for Cyberspace http://www.defense.gov/news/d20110714cyber.pdf

2. Department of Defense Quadrennial Defense Review http://www.defense.gov/pubs/2014_Quadrennial_Defense_Review.pdf

3. AIR FORCE INSTRUCTION 10-1701 COMMAND AND CONTROL
(C2) FOR CYBERSPACE OPERATIONS http://www.fas.org/irp/doddir/usaf/afi10-1701.pdf

4. Aftergood, Steven. U.S. Military Given Secret "Execute Order" on Cyber Operations Secrecy News March 13, 2014 http://blogs.fas.org/secrecy/2014/03/execute-order/

5. DIA Transcript of Worldwide Threat Assessment http://www.dia.mil/News/SpeechesandTestimonies/tabid/7031/Article/13225/worldwide-threat-assessment.aspx

6. Bumiller, Elisabeth and Shanker, Thom, "Panetta Warns of Dire Threat of Cyberattack on U.S."
New York Times, 11 October 2012

CHAPTER FIFTEEN

1. Anderson, Mark "Rooting out malware with a side channel chip defense system" *IEEE Spectrum* 27 Jan 2015 http:// spectrum.ieee.org/riskfactor/computing/hardware/rooting-out-malware-with-a-sidechannel-chip-defense-system

2. Trusted Internet Connections (TIC) Initiative Statement of Capability Evaluation Report http://download.101com.com/pub/gcn/newspics/TICstatus-report.pdf

CHAPTER SIXTEEN

1. Numoto, Takeshi "Microsoft acquires Aorato to give enterprise customers better defense against digital intruders in a hybrid cloud world" November 13, 2014 http://blogs.microsoft.com/blog/2014/11/13/microsoft-acquires-aorato-give-enterprise-customers-better-defense-digital-intruders-hybrid-cloud-world/

The Growing Catalog at IT-Harvest Press

IT-Harvest Press is a small press publisher of non-fiction. We look for authors who are accomplished writers with an on-line presence. A common theme in our publications is the combination of history, policy, and technology.

www.ith-press.com

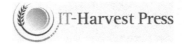